CHRISTIAN BASICS 101:

A HANDB00K ON CHRISTIAN GROWTH

Frank R. Shivers

PRESS

Copyright © 2009, 2010 by Frank R. Shivers

Christian Basics 101:
A Handbook on Christian Growth
by Frank R. Shivers

Printed in the United States of America
Library of Congress Cataloging - in - Publication Data

Library of Congress Control Number: 2008910967
ISBN 978-1-60791-296-5

Unless otherwise indicated, Bible quotations are taken from The Holy Bible *King James Version.*

Cover design by Click-Graphics
Editor: Dan Hazlett

For information
P.O. Box 9991
Columbia, South Carolina 29290
www.frankshivers.com

Other Volumes in this Series
The Evangelistic Invitation 101
Evangelistic Preaching 101
Soulwinning 101
Revivals 101

www.xulonpress.com

To Dr. Kenneth W. Ridings
For giving freely of himself to the task of mentoring
young preacher-boys at Fruitland Bible Institute
in excess of forty years as President, Professor,
Preacher and Pattern.

CONTENTS

INTRODUCTION

I fear as C.H. Spurgeon said, "Many Christians remain stunted and dwarfed in spiritual things, so as to present the same appearance year after year. No up-springing of advanced and refined feeling is manifest in them. They exist but do not 'grow up into him in all things.'" (Spurgeon, Morning, Oct. 20) Christian growth is *work*. Paul emphasized this fact in Philippians 2:12, stating, "Work out your own salvation with fear and trembling." The words *work out* are used by the First Century author Strabo to refer to digging silver out of silver mines, a task that required diligent and exhausting labor. The Christian is to *dig out* of his salvation its fullest blessings, beliefs and benefits. "Let your roots grow down into him, and let your lives be built on him. Then your faith will grow strong in the truth you were taught, and you will overflow with thankfulness." (Colossians 2:4, NLT) Peter admonishes, "Add to your faith virtue" or, as another translation renders, "Furnish your faith with resolution." (2 Peter 1:5) Commenting on this verse, Oswald Chambers stated, "'Add' means to get in the habit of doing things, and in the initial stages it is difficult. To take the initiative is to make a beginning, to instruct yourself in the way you have to go." (Chambers, May 10) You were saved in a twinkling of an eye the moment you confessed Christ as Lord and Savior but it will take months or years of *heart work* to mature in the faith.

The following studies are designed to give assistance in this *work*. The first chapter includes foundational Christian beliefs that are paramount for spiritual growth. Subsequent chapters deal with the New Birth, the Church, Prayer, Bible Study, Baptism, the Lord's Supper, Stewardship, Satan, Witnessing, Key Bible Words, Overview of the Bible and The "Neglect Not's" of Growth. Work through each study prayerfully and thoroughly.

The Apostle Paul's aspiration was "to know Him (Christ) and the power of his resurrection, and the fellowship of his sufferings, being made conformable unto his death." (Philippians 3:10) He knew Christ as Savior and Lord, but he longed to know Him more intimately; this he pursued continuously. The verb "know" means "to know by experience" revealing Paul would not be content with simple head knowledge or second-hand knowledge of Christ. Is Paul's aspiration yours? Do you hunger and thirst to know Christ more intimately? Let this be your focus, not on how much sin you can avoid or how much good you can do. Spiritual disciplines simply become legalistic weights if engaged without their purpose being to propel a believer to know Christ more devotedly. It is important that Christians keep the main thing the main thing.

The two ways to make tea illustrates the two methods of spiritual growth. The first is to boil water and dip the tea bag in and out of the water until ready. The second is to boil water and simply place the tea bag in the water until ready. Don't be the type of believer who dips in and out of the church, Bible study, prayer, service, and fellowship with Christ but be the type who *abides* (stays put) in these without wavering. (John 15:4 -7)

The London pastor C. H. Spurgeon said, "The longer I live, the more sure do I become that our happiness in life, our comfort in trouble, and our strength for service all depend upon our living near to God, nay, dwelling in God, as the lilies in the water. . .I would rather spend an hour in the presence of the Lord than a century in prosperity without Him... He who lives without prayer, he who lives with little prayer, he who seldom reads the Word, and he who seldom looks up to heaven for a fresh influence from on high—he will be the man whose heart will become dry and barren. However, he who falls in secret on his God, who spends much time in holy retirement, who delights to meditate on the words of the Most High, and whose soul is given up to Christ—such a man must have an overflowing heart. As his heart is, such will his life be." (helives.com)

Marie Barnett capsulized a heart of intimacy for Christ all believers should exhibit when she wrote

And I, I'm desperate for You,
And I, I'm lost without You.
Oh Lord, I'm lost without You. I'm lost without You.
This is the air I breathe; this is the air I breathe
Your Holy presence living in me.

Christian Basics 101 is designed for pastor classes, Sunday School programs, and Camp/Retreat curriculums. It also may be individually distributed to new believers or church members for personal study. *Digging Deeper* questions are included at the conclusion of each chapter to maximize comprehension and application.

It is my prayer these studies will richly bless, instruct and enable the believers' spiritual growth. "But grow in grace, and in the knowledge of our Lord and Savior Jesus Christ. To him be glory both now and for ever." (2 Peter 3:18)

Frank Shivers

1

THIS WE BELIEVE

"My people are destroyed for a lack of knowledge." (Hosea 4:6)

"It is a great thing to begin the Christian life by believing good solid doctrine. Some people have received twenty different "gospels" in as many years; how many more they will accept before they get to their journey's end, it would be difficult to predict. I thank God that He early taught me the gospel, and I have been so perfectly satisfied with it, that I do not want to know any other." C.H. Spurgeon (Spurgeon, Autobiography, 167)

A foundational understanding of biblical theology (doctrinal beliefs) is essential to the maturing Christian. Doctrinal deficiency results in spiritual illiteracy and stunted growth. C.H. Spurgeon stated, "Believe what you do believe, or else you will never persuade anybody else to believe it." (Comfort, Ray 245)

John Stott remarked, "The devil disturbs the church as much by error as by evil. When he cannot entice Christian people into sin, he deceives them with false doctrine." (Stott,

The Message of Galatians, 24) The English poet Samuel Taylor Coleridge spoke of "truths often considered as so true that they lose the power of truth and lie bedridden in the dormitory of the soul." (Coleridge 117) The foundational tenets of the Christian faith are such truths and need "awakening" to fresh meaning and reality.

It is imperative the Christian know what he believes and why he believes it so he can "be ready always to *give* an answer to every man that asketh you a reason of the hope that is in you with meekness and fear." (1 Peter 3:15) In this chapter a simple and concise presentation of core Christian beliefs on which to build a thorough and biblically sound theology is presented.

THIS WE BELIEVE ABOUT GOD

God is *Omnipotent*. He is all-powerful. God can do anything He wants to do, and no man or nation can stop Him. C.H. Spurgeon stated, "God's power is like Himself, self-existent, self-sustained. He is Himself the great central source and originator of all power." (Pink, Attributes, Chapter 9) God is *Omniscient*. He is all-knowing. There is nothing of which God is unaware. Has it ever occurred to you that nothing has ever occurred to God? God is *Omnipresent*. He is present everywhere at the same time. God is *immutable*. He remains ever the same. "Jesus Christ the same yesterday, and today, and forever." (Hebrews 13:8) God is *love*. God loves man and desires him to be saved. (John 3:16) This love of God is uninfluenced by anything man has done or may do and is never ending. "We love Him because He first loved us." (I John 4:19) God is *holy* and *righteous* incapable of doing wrong or failing to do as He declares. (Isaiah 6:3) God is creator, owner and *sustainer* of all that exists. (Colossians 1:16-17)

The Trinity

Christians do not believe in three Gods but in one God in three persons. Augustine said regarding the doctrine of the Trinity, "In no other subject is error more dangerous, inquiry more laborious, or the discovery of truth more rewarding." (Augustine 19) The 2000 Baptist Faith and Message stated, "The eternal triune God reveals Himself to us as Father, Son, and Holy Spirit, with distinct personal attributes, but without division of nature, essence, or being." God is three persons in one nature: God the Father, God the Son, and God the Holy Spirit simultaneously – the Trinity. Norman Geisler stated, "There is only one 'What' (essence) in God, but there are three 'Whos' (persons) in that one 'What.'" (Geisler, Systematic Theology Vol 2, 279) D.L. Moody illustrated the Trinity by stating that God is like a triangle which is one figure, yet with three different sides at the same time. Patrick of Ireland used a shamrock to explain the Trinity. In holding up a shamrock he would ask the people, "Is it one leaf or three?" "It is both one leaf and three they would reply." "And it is so with God" he would conclude. C.H. Spurgeon stated, "Mark the union of the Three Divine Persons in all their gracious acts. How unwisely do those believers talk who make preferences in the Persons of the Trinity; who think of Jesus as if he were the embodiment of everything lovely and gracious, while the Father they regard as severely just, but destitute of kindness. Equally wrong are those who magnify the decree of the Father, and the atonement of the Son, so as to depreciate the work of the Spirit. In deeds of grace none of the Persons of the Trinity act apart from the rest. They are as united in their deeds as in their essence. In their love towards the chosen they are one, and in the actions which flow from that great central source they are still undivided." (Spurgeon, Morning, July 12) The word "Trinity" does not occur in the Bible, but the Trinitarian doctrine is revealed in such texts as Genesis 1:26; 3:22; Numbers 6: 24 – 26;

Isaiah 48: 16; Matthew 28: 19; 2 Corinthians 13:14; John 14:25–31; 1 John 5:6–8. This doctrine is simply *presented* in scripture, not *explained*. It is *authenticated* overwhelmingly in the biblical text.

THIS WE BELIEVE ABOUT THE BIBLE

The Bible is unique. There is no other book like it. The Bible is God's only written revelation to man. It was written by 40 men over a period of 1500 years. The Bible consists of 66 books, 39 in the Old Testament and 27 in the New Testament. The Bible is the first book to be printed and more copies of it have been printed than any other book. (Smith, William) It is totally true in fact and doctrine. It has no contradictions. It is trustworthy. "Through the Holy Spirit's agency, God is involved in both the production and interpretation of Scripture. Men of God in antiquity spoke as they were moved by the Holy Spirit. 'Moved' means literally 'to bear along.' Scripture is infallible precisely because the Holy Spirit 'bore along' the prophets who spoke and wrote." (I Peter 1: 20-21) (Criswell, Study Bible 1459)

Charles C. Ryrie commented, "More than 5,000 manuscripts of the New Testament exist today, which makes the New Testament the best-attested document of all ancient writings. The contrast is quite startling." (Ryrie Study Bible 1991) Lewis S. Chafer stated regarding the Bible that "Man could not write such a Book if he would." (Chafer 27)

What was the criterion for the inclusion (canonicity) of the 66 books in the Bible and the exclusion of others? Under God's leadership, selection was based upon a book's being divinely inspired. Paige Patterson stated, "The sole criterion of the canon (*straightedge, ruler or measuring rod)* of Scripture is inspiration (2 Timothy 3:16-17), God's testimony through the Holy Spirit." (Criswell, Criswell Study Bible, XVII) Books that were written by apostles under the inspiration of the Holy Spirit alone were accepted to frame the Bible, and all others were rejected. B. B. Warfield remarked, "And in every case the principle on which a book was accepted, or doubts against it laid aside, was the historical tradition of apostolicity." (Warfield) The basic principle of book inclusion for the New Testament "is identical to that of the Old Testament, since it narrows down to a matter of divine inspiration. Whether we think of the prophets of Old Testament times or the apostles and their God-given associates of the New, the recognition at the very time of their writing that they were authentic spokesmen for God is what determines the intrinsic canonicity of their writing. It is altogether God's Word only if it is God-breathed. We can be assured that the books under question were received by the church of the apostolic age precisely when they had been certified by an apostle as being thus inspired." (Comfort, Philip 172)

In the early church false writings were being distributed that clearly were not divinely inspired of God as claimed because they "preached another Jesus" (2 Corinthians 11:4) or consisted of fabricated content. These books were rejected from inclusion in the Bible. Francis Dixon of the Landsdowne Bible School and Postal Fellowship, wrote, "There is not one single proved inaccuracy in the whole Bible. The Bible is accurate historically, geographically, genealogically, scientifically, psychologically, typologically and verbally." (Dixon June 9, 1964)

The writer of Hebrews stated, "The Word of God is quick, and powerful, and sharper than any two-edged sword, piercing even to the dividing asunder of soul and spirit and of the joints and marrow, and is a discerner of the thoughts and intents of the heart." (Hebrews 4:12) The Bible is fully alive. It is life giving communication from God to man. It has power to convict man of sin and bring him to God. No other book in the world can do that. John Stott stated, "There is no saving power in the words of men. The devil does not relinquish his grasp upon his prisoners at the bidding of mere mortals. No word has authority for him but the Word of God." (Stott, The Preacher's Portrait, 100) Nothing is in the Bible that shouldn't be, and nothing is missing that ought to be. "The B – I – B – L – E, yes it's the Book for me. I stand alone on the Word of God. The B-I-B-L-E." Believe it against the opinion of any scientist, teacher, preacher, or friend. It is the Word of Him who cannot lie. D.L. Moody remarked, "When Christ said, 'The Scriptures cannot be broken' He meant every word He said. Devil and man and hell have been in league for centuries to try to break the Word of God, but they can not do it. If you get it for your footing, you have a good footing, for time and eternity. 'Heaven and earth shall pass away, but my Word shall not pass away.' My friends, that Word is going to live, and there is no power in perdition or in earth to blot it out." (Moody, Pleasures and Profit, 32 -33) Jonathan Edwards rightly wrote: "Spiritual understanding sees what is actually in Scripture; it does not make a new meaning for it. Making a new meaning for Scripture is equivalent to making a new Scripture! It is adding to God's Word, a practice God condemns (Proverbs 30:6)…A large part of the false religion in the world is made up of…experiences and the false notion they excite. Non-Christian religions are full of them. So (unfortunately) is the history of the Church. These experiences captivate people so Satan transforms himself into an angel of light, deceives multitudes, and corrupts true religion. Church leaders must be constantly on their guard against these delusions." (Edwards 89-90)

W.A. Criswell in Why I Preach that the Bible is Literally True stated, "Jesus believed and taught the infallibility of Scripture. He regarded it as divine authority and as the final court of appeal concerning all questions. He sets His seal to its historicity and its revelation from God. He supplements it, but never supplants it. He amplifies it, but He never nullifies it. He modifies it according to His own divine prerogative, He fulfills it according to His divine mission, but He never lessens its divine authority. His attitude towards the Scripture was one of total trust. It was the direct written Word of God to man." (Criswell, Why I Preach, 19-20) The Bible is not simply to be believed, but it is to be applied to one's life. (James 1:22)

R.G. Lee stated, "All of this Book I believe. Not some of it, not most of it, not part of it, but ALL of it! Inspired in totality, the Miracle Book of diversity and unity of harmony and infinite complexity." (Lee 178)

"The Bible is God's self-disclosure, the divine autobiography. In the Bible the subject and the object are identical, for in it God is speaking about God. He makes himself known progressively in the rich variety of his being: as the Creator of the universe and of human beings in his own image, the climax of his creation; as the living God who sustains and animates everything he has made; as the covenant God who chose Abraham, Isaac, Jacob and their descendants to be his special people; and as a gracious God who is slow to anger and quick to forgive, but also as a righteous God who punishes idolatry and injustice among his own people as well as in the pagan nations. Then in the New Testament he reveals himself as the Father of our Lord and Savior Jesus Christ, who sent him into the world to take our nature upon him, to be born and grow, live and teach, work and suffer, die and rise, occupy the throne and send the Holy Spirit; next as the God of the new covenant community; the church, who sends his people into the world as his witnesses and his servants in the power of the Holy Spirit; and finally as the God who one day will send Jesus Christ in power and glory to save, to judge and to reign, who will create a new universe, and who in the end will be everything to everybody." (Stott, You Can Trust, 69)

See Chapter Twelve for an overview of the Bible including a synopsis of each book.

THIS WE BELIEVE ABOUT SIN AND SATAN

Sin entered the human race in the Garden of Eden when Adam and Eve disobeyed God. Scripture states, "Wherefore, as by one man sin entered into the world, and death by sin; and so death passed upon all men, for that all have sinned." (Romans 5:12) Sin is failure to keep God's law (Exodus 20) and any act that does not glorify God. (1 Corinthians 10:31) Sin is disobedience to the will of God, it results in separation from God presently and eternally, and "All have sinned." (Romans 3:23)

Satan's name was Lucifer before his fall (Isaiah 14:12) due to pride (Ezekiel 28:17). He was the anointed cherub of God. (Ezekiel 28:14) He possesses intelligence (2 Corinthians 2:11); memory (Matthew 4:6); a will (2 Timothy 2:26); a desire (Luke 22:31); wrath (Revelation 12:12); and great organizational ability (I Timothy 4:1; Revelation 2:9, 24). Satan's purpose is to usurp God's authority in the world by deceiving, lying, tempting and destroying. (John 10: 10) Unlike God Satan is not omnipresent. He has at his disposal legions of demons ("unclean spirits"; "evil spirits"; "deceiving spirits") to deploy throughout the earth to antagonize and attack the believer. (Matthew 10:1; Acts 19: 12-13; I Timothy 4:1; Revelation 16:14) One of the primary purposes of Jesus' coming to earth was to overthrow Satan's power (Matthew 12:25 -29; John 12:31), casting him and his demons into eternal damnation in the Lake of Fire and Brimstone. (Matthew 25:41; Revelation 20:10) Hell was created for Satan and his demons, not man. All people, however, who live alienated from God in rebellion and unbelief will suffer this eternal punishment. God longs for all to be saved so that none experience the torment of Hell.

(2 Peter 3:9) The believer is promised victory over Satan's tactics. (I John 4:4)

THIS WE BELIEVE ABOUT SALVATION

God loved the world so much that He sent His only son to die upon a Cross to make possible sin's forgiveness. (John 3:16) Nothing short of Jesus' death, burial and resurrection can atone (forgive) for man's sin. It is when man repents of sin (expresses godly sorrow for the sin of rejecting Christ and changes his mind about the role of Christ in his life) and exhibits faith (personal trust) in Jesus Christ that he is saved. (Acts 20:21) Salvation is a free gift of God available to all people that cannot be merited, earned or deserved. (Ephesians 2:8-9)

John MacArthur remarked, "If we believe the Bible, we cannot concede that other religions might be true as well. If we believe that Christ is Lord of all, and if we truly love Him, we cannot countenance the doctrines of those who deny Him. (1 Corinthians 16:22) Christianity, if true at all, is exclusively true. Inherent in the claims of Christ is the assertion that He alone offers truth, and all religious systems that deviate from His truth are false. Jesus said, "I am the way, the truth, and the life; no one comes to the Father, but through me." (John 14:6) If this is true, every other religion is a lie. (Romans 3:4)" (MacArthur, Truth Matters, 71)

THIS WE BELIEVE ABOUT ETERNAL SECURITY

A person "Born Again" into the family of God can never be "unborn." (John 5:24) Jesus' promise of abundant and eternal life to all that repent and believe is certain (John 10:10; Acts 20:21) and trustworthy. Satan may attack and assault the believers' faith but he can never steal it. He can never undo what God did in salvation. At the moment of salvation, the believer's name is written with permanent ink in the Lamb's Book of Life and neither Satan, Demons, nor man can erase it. (Romans 8:31-39)

Jesus teaches in John 6:37 that all who come to Him in repentance and faith are saved and that they are saved permanently. In John 6:39-40 Jesus states that He will not lose anyone who is added to the Kingdom by the New Birth. The Apostle Peter declares that the Christian is "kept by the power of God" unto salvation. (I Peter 1:5) God's omnipotent and supreme power is well able to keep the believers' faith secure. John MacArthur stated, "No one can steal the Christian's treasure, and no one can disqualify him from receiving it." (MacArthur, Study Bible, I Peter 1:5) Jesus emphatically declares that His sheep (the saved) would "never perish." (John 3:16) Never means never. In Philippians 1:6, the Apostle Paul affirms that the saving work God initiated in the believer He will see through until its completion in Heaven. The strongest proof for eternal security in the entire Bible is John 10:28-29, which states that under no circumstance can a believer be snatched out of the encompassing hand of God. Explaining I Corinthians 12:13, Charles Ryrie stated, "At conversion the believer is joined to the body of Christ by the Baptism of the Holy Spirit. If salvation can be lost, then one would have to be severed from the body and Christ's body would then be dismembered." (Geisler, Systematic Theology Vol. 3, 309) This is an impossibility.

The Christian can and does sin. (I John 2:1) This is due to his dualistic nature, the flesh (carnal) and the spirit (spiritual). These two wrestle one another seeking dominion throughout the believer's life. It is when the believer yields to the carnal nature and the lusts of the old man that sin results. Divine discipline may be exacted for the rebellious act, but his salvation is never in jeopardy. (Romans 8:1) The Apostle Paul experienced this inner struggle between the two natures like every other Christian (Romans 7: 15-25) and discovered that the appetites of the flesh can only be thwarted by walking in the fullness of the Holy Spirit. (Romans 8: 1-11) A native attempting to explain to a missionary the inner struggles of the flesh warring against the spirit said it was like two dogs fighting constantly. When asked which dog wins, the native replied, "The one I feed the most." In the warfare of the soul against the flesh "the one you feed the most" will win. Habits good or bad exist due to personal cultivation. J.I. Packer commented, "Sometimes the regenerate backslide and fall into gross sin. But in this they act out of character, do violence to their own new nature, and make themselves deeply miserable, so that eventually they seek and find restoration to righteousness. In retrospect, their lapse seems to them to have been madness. When regenerate believers act in character, they manifest a humble, grateful desire to please the God who saved them; and the knowledge that he is pledged to keep them safe forever simply increases this desire." (Packer, Concise Theology, 180)

The fact of Eternal Security does not give a license to sin. (Romans 6:15) In truth, the person genuinely saved both desires and delights in avoiding sin and is crushed deeply when he commits sin. In reality, many who profess to be saved but live contrary to the teaching of the Bible are not saved (Matthew 7: 22-23) but are merely members of the visible church rather than the invisible Church. The Apostle John wrote of such, "They went out from us, but they were not of us; for if they had been of us, they would *no doubt* have continued with us: but *they went out*, that they might be made manifest that they were not all of us." (I John 2:19)

THIS WE BELIEVE ABOUT THE HOLY SPIRIT

The enabling and illuminating power source of the Christian's life is the Holy Spirit. (Acts 1:8) The Holy Spirit is the third person of the Trinity and resides in the believer. (1 Corinthians 3:16–17; 6:19–20) The Holy Spirit helps the believer to pray (Romans 8:26–27); avoid doing wrong

(Galatians 5:16); tell others of Jesus (Acts 1:8); understand the Bible (1 Corinthians 2:6–16); live in peace and joy (Romans 5:5); know comfort in sorrow and difficulty (John 14:16–17); and discern the Will of God (Job 32:8; 33:4) There is but one baptism of the Holy Spirit and that occurs at conversion, but there can and should be many infillings of the Holy Spirit throughout the Christian's life. (Ephesians 5:17) The Baptism of the Holy Spirit is when the Holy Spirit takes up residence in the Christian at salvation; the infilling of the Holy Spirit is when the Christian yields to His control allowing Him not only to be resident but President in his life. (Galatians 5:16, 25) Referring to the infilling of the Holy Spirit in the believer's life, Leonard Ravenhill stated, "An automobile will never move until it has ignition-fire; so some men are neither moved nor moving because they have everything but fire." (Ravenhill 114) The Holy Spirit ignites the Christian and "fires the engine" in the Christian's devotion, duty, and discipline.

C.H. Spurgeon stated, "God has provided the Holy Spirit to guide us. (John 16:13) The Holy Spirit is infallible. He knows everything and cannot lead us astray. He is ever-present. When we have no commentator or minister to help us, we still have the Holy Spirit. The Holy Spirit teaches us in three ways: suggestion, direction and illumination. There are thoughts that dwell in our minds that are suggestions put there by the Spirit for us to follow. Sometimes He leads us by direction, leading our thoughts along into a more excellent channel than that which we started. Sometimes He leads us by illuminating the Word of God to us." (Spurgeon, "Holy Ghost")

THIS WE BELIEVE ABOUT LAST THINGS

Jesus promised to return for His bride, the church of the redeemed. (John 14:1-6) An airline passenger may purchase either a one-way ticket or a two-way ticket. Obviously, the first indicates the passenger's desire to remain at the ticketed destination while the latter shows his desire to visit the ticketed destination but to return to the originating city at a stated time and date. John informs the believer that Jesus has a *two-way ticket.* (Revelation 22:20) The time and date for Jesus' return for the Church is set but known only to God. "But of that day and hour knoweth no *man*, no, not the angels of heaven, but my Father only." (Matthew 24:36) There are in excess of 320 references to the Second Coming in the Bible. One of every twenty-five verses in the New Testament reference this event. These references include Matthew 24:30; 2 Thessalonians 1:7 - 8; Matthew 25:31; 1 Thessalonians 5: 2 - 3; Matthew 25:31; Titus 2:13; Matthew 24: 42 -51; and 1Thessalonians 4: 13 -18.

The Rapture (I Thessalonians 4:13-18; I Corinthians 15:51-58)

The word "rapture" means "to seize quickly or suddenly; to transport to a state of happiness." Biblically the Rapture is the event that occurs upon Jesus' return for His bride, that of "catching up" to Heaven the saints and making complete their salvation. The first to be "caught up" with Him in the air are the saved dead; following, then, will be the living saints. "For the Lord himself shall descend from heaven with a shout, with the voice of the archangel, and with the trump of God: and the dead in Christ shall rise first: Then we which are alive *and* remain shall be caught up together with them in the clouds, to meet the Lord in the air: and so shall we ever be with the Lord." (I Thessalonians 4: 16-17)

The Second Coming of Christ

There are two phases of the coming of Christ. The first is the "Rapture" in which Jesus comes *for* the saints and meets them in the *air*. It is at this time the saint will be changed in a twinkling of an eye to be like Jesus (I Corinthians 15: 51-52), receive rewards at the Judgment Seat (I Corinthians 4:5), and *partake* of the Marriage Supper of the Lamb. (Revelation 19:7–10) The second phase is when He comes *with* His saints to *earth* to set up His Kingdom of 1000 years, known as the Millennium reign. (Revelation 19:11–15) D.L. Moody, the great evangelist, remarked, "I have felt like working three times as hard ever since I came to understand that my Lord was coming back again." (Moody, Great Preaching on the Second Coming, 109) The Christian should feel this same way.

The Judgment of Saint and Sinner
There will be a day when the people who love Jesus and those who do not will face God's judgment. In every courtroom in America there is a Judge who sits on a bench and makes people accept responsibility for their actions. God will do the same. (Hebrews 9:27) The Bible does not speak of a general judgment for all mankind. There will be two judgments, one for the believer (Judgment Seat of Christ, 2 Corinthians 5: 9-10) and one for the unbeliever (Great White Throne, Revelation 20: 11-15). The Christian is not judged with regard to salvation because his soul is eternally secured through the blood of Christ; the Christian is judged in regard to conduct and service. (1 Corinthians 3: 11-15) Results of this judgment determine one's reward. (Revelation 22:12; 4:10) The Bible states at least five rewards the believer may receive: The Crown of Life for the persecuted saint who endures suffering for the cause of Christ (Revelation 2:10); The Crown of Rejoicing for the soul winner (I Thessalonians 2:19; Philippians 4:1); The Crown of Righteousness for believers who look for Jesus' return (2 Timothy 4:8); The Crown of Glory will be given to pastors who faithfully proclaim Christ and Him crucified, feed the flock of God, exhibit spiritual oversight for the flock of God and lead by worthy example (I Peter 5:1-4); and The Incorruptible Crown will be awarded the believer who, as an athlete, disciplines

his body into subjection to Christ and becomes victorious over the flesh and who faithfully runs the Christian race to the finish line (I Corinthians 9:24-27). John declares that the believer's reward is forfeitable (2 John 8) by failing to run the Christian race by the rules as presented in the Word of God. The unbeliever at the Great White Throne will be judged according to his sin and rejection of Christ as Lord and Savior and will receive the condemnation of eternal torment in Hell. (Revelation 21:8)

Heaven and Hell

The Bible speaks of two eternal literal abodes, Heaven and Hell. (Luke 16: 22-23)

Heaven is a *place of Reception* by Jesus. Jesus, not an angel, will greet and meet the believer at Heaven's door. (John 14:3) Seeing and being with Jesus for all eternity is Heaven. "I have formerly lived by hearsay and faith," said Bunyan's Mr. Stand-fast, "but now I go where I shall live by sight, and shall be with him, in whose company I delight myself." (Packer, Growing in Christ, 88) Heaven is a *place of Reunion* with saints. The saint will fellowship with not only redeemed parents, children, grandparents, friends known but also with the host of the redeemed unknown like the prophets, disciples, patriarchs, missionaries and evangelists. (I Corinthians 13:12) Heaven is a *place of Release.* It is "Hallelujah Square" because everybody is healthy and happy, having been freed from the grip of pain, sickness, crippling illness, suffering, and the constant pull of Satan toward sin. (Revelation 21:4) Heaven is a *place of Rest.* It has been said a person enters this world crying and goes out sighing. The saint gets tired and worn with the demands of livelihood and battling the foes of darkness, but "a day of rest" (Hebrews 4:9) is coming for the redeemed when he "will lay down his sword and shield down by the riverside and study war no more." A Christian works on knowing soon the labor will end with eternal rest in the Father's presence. "The more I get older," Billy Graham stated, "the more I get closer to (death), the happier I am. I am filled with anticipation – I'm looking forward to it. One reason is, I'll get some rest!" (Graham, Life Wisdom, 105) Heaven is a *place of Rejoicing*. (Revelation 5: 11-12) In Heaven, the saint's joy will overflow into a song of praise and adoration to the King for making salvation possible. On earth, mankind is plagued with troubles and disappointments that rob joy and peace, but this is not so in Heaven. Paul Little declared, "Heaven will not be the boring experience of strumming a harp on a cloud, as some facetiously characterize it. It will be the most dynamic, expanding, exhilarating experience conceivable. Our problem now is that, with our finite minds, we cannot imagine it." (Little 189) Heaven is a *place of Reward*. (Revelation 22:12) This subject is discussed in *The Judgment of Saint and Sinner* in this chapter. Heaven is a *place of Responsibility*. Heaven is a place not only of worship but also of work. Christians will serve God in various ways for all eternity. (Revelation 22:3) J.I. Packer commented, "What shall we do in heaven? Not lounge around!-but worship, work, think, and communicate, enjoying activity, beauty, people, and God." (Packer, Growing in Christ, 88) C.H. Spurgeon stated, "It is a sweet thing to die in the Lord: it is a covenant-blessing to sleep in Jesus. Death is no longer banishment, it is a return from exile, a going home to the many mansions where the loved ones already dwell." (Spurgeon, Morning, April 20)

Hell is the complete opposite. The narrative of the rich man and Lazarus told by Jesus reveals Hell's sordid nature. (Luke 16: 19-31) Hell is a *place of Pain*. (vv. 23-24) Physical and mental torment unimaginable will be experienced in Hell. Scripture makes clear that there will be varying degrees of punishment inflicted in Hell. (Matthew 10:15; 11:22, 24; Mark 6:11; Hebrews 10:29) Hell is a *place of Passion*. (v 24) Insatiable appetites and desires plague the inhabitants of

Hell forever and ever. Hell is a *place of Parting.* (v 26) The unsaved are forever separated from the redeemed. Hell is a *place of Prayer.* (v 27) The eternally damned will come to see the need of God but woefully too late. Hell is a domain in which man with weeping, wailing, and gnashing of teeth cry out to God for salvation but in vain. Hell is a *place of Permeating Darkness.* Jude describes Hell as "the blackness of darkness forever." (Jude 13) Utter blackness makes relationships impossible in Hell. C.S. Lewis declared Hell is a place of "nothing but yourself for all eternity!" (sermoncentral.com) The inhabitants of Hell only know isolation and utter loneliness; there are no friendships or fellowship. Hell is a *place of Permanence.* (v 26) Hell hath "No Exits." There is no way out of Hell so there is no hope for its inhabitants. However, the worst part of Hell is that it is a place where God is not! God does not desire any person to go to Hell. (2 Peter 3:9)

R.A. Torrey remarked, "A man's usefulness or uselessness depends upon what he believes and the stand he takes on the facts of Hell. But a man who accepts that part of the Bible which he wants to accept and which he calls agreeable to his thinking, and rejects that part which he does not want to accept, in plain, unvarnished language, is a fool!" (Great Preaching on Christ 175)

John Stott stated, "Many suppose that intellectual freedom is identical with 'free thought,' that is, the liberty to think and believe absolutely anything you want to think and believe. But this is not freedom. To believe nothing is to be in bondage to meaninglessness. To believe lies is to be in bondage to falsehood. True intellectual freedom is found in believing the truth and living by it." (Stott, The Bible and Crisis, 14)

References on Biblical Doctrine
A Survey of Bible Doctrine, Charles C. Ryrie
What Baptists Believe, Herschel H. Hobbs
Know What You Believe, Paul Little
The Popular Bible Prophecy Commentary, Tim LaHaye and Ed Hindson
Systematic Theology (Volumes 1-4), Norman Geisler

Digging Deeper
1. What are the seven attributes of God discussed in this chapter?
2. Why is the Bible trustworthy?
3. What is sin and its ultimate consequence?
4. What is Satan's purpose?
5. What are the two conditions of salvation? (Acts 20:21)
6. Explain Jesus' teaching on Eternal Security.
7. Explain the role of the Holy Spirit in the believer's life?
8. Contrast the Baptism of the Spirit with the infilling of the Spirit.
9. Share the biblical perspective of Last Things.
10. What are the Five Rewards for believers?

2

THE NEW BIRTH

"The doctrine of the New Birth upsets all false religion- all false views about the Bible and about God." D.L. Moody (Moody, "Way to God")

"There must be true and deep conviction of sin. This the preacher must labor to produce, for where this is not felt, the new birth has not taken place." C.H. Spurgeon (Lawrence 430)

Years ago, someone wrote a poem entitled "The Land of Beginning Again." The writer sighed for a land where he could lay aside his past, much the same way a man puts aside his soiled clothes, and start life afresh. This "Land of Beginning Again" is found in a personal relationship with Jesus Christ that the Bible calls "The New Birth." This spiritual birth involves "repentance and faith." (Acts 20:21) Repentance is godly sorrow over wrongdoing, coupled with a desire to change. Faith is belief in the fact and meaning of Jesus' death, burial and resurrection and receiving Jesus into one's life as both Lord and Savior. (Romans 10: 9 -13) Based upon these two conditions of salvation, at the time of sincere prayer to receive Christ as Lord and Savior a sinner is "Born

Again." (Romans 10:13; Revelation 3:20) God's promises assure this fact. (I John 1:9; Titus 1:2)

C.H. Spurgeon remarked, "This great work is supernatural. It is not an operation which a man performs for himself: a new principle is infused, which works in the heart, renews the soul, and affects the entire man. It is not a change of my name, but a renewal of my nature, so that I am not the man I used to be, but a new man in Christ Jesus." (Spurgeon, Morning, March 6) Prior to the Civil War, Abraham Lincoln purchased an African-American woman. He immediately told her former master, "Remove her chains." The woman asked Lincoln, "What ya' goin' to do wit' me now?" He responded, "Why I am going to set you free." "Free, what do ya mean free?" she asked. Lincoln replied, "I mean you are a free person. You are no longer a slave." He went on to explain to her that she could go wherever and do whatever she wanted. The lady to his shock shouted, "Then I want to be wit' you!" Puzzled, he looked down at her and said, "You can go anywhere. Why would you want to follow me?" The rescued woman answered, "Cause I wanna be wit' the one who set me free." Every person that experiences the deliverance of Jesus Christ from the power and penalty of sin feels that same way toward Him.

Religion is not synonymous with the New Birth

Church attendance, moral living, religious service, baptism, and partaking of the Lord's Supper are not synonymous with the New Birth. The believer does these things because he is a child of God, not in order to become a child of God. These things are the 'fruit' of salvation not the root of salvation. Possessing a *False Hope* of salvation is as equally damning as that of a *No Hope*. Jesus warns, "Not every one that saith unto me, Lord, Lord, shall enter into the kingdom of heaven; but he that doeth the will of my Father which is in heaven. Many will say to me in that day, Lord,

Lord, have we not prophesied in thy name? and in thy name have cast out devils? and in thy name done many wonderful works? And then will I profess unto them, I never knew you: depart from me, ye that work iniquity." (Matthew 7: 21 – 23) Salvation is totally based upon Christ's work for the sinner at Calvary; man cannot add to it in even the minutest way.

John Piper, in an article entitled "The Agonizing Problem of the Assurance of Salvation," stated, "This boils down to whether I have saving faith. What makes this agonizing for many in the history of the church and today is that there are people who think they have saving faith but don't. (Matthew 7: 21-22) So the agonizing question for some is: Do I really have saving faith? Is my faith real? Am I self-deceived?" Piper cited how sincere, well-meaning people in an effort to gain assurance wrongly believe that faith is a mere decision to affirm biblical truths, like that of Jesus being the Son of God who died for man's sin or that faith requires no life-change to demonstrate its reality. Regarding such efforts, he stated, "But these strategies to help assurance backfire. And, perhaps worst of all, they sometimes give assurance to people who should not have it." (Piper)

Base Salvation upon Fact not Feeling

Feelings are not proof of salvation. Base the proof of salvation upon God's Word. Certainly the believer should experience feelings of relief that things are eternally settled with God and of awesome gratitude to God, but to validate salvation based upon emotional experiences is unbiblical. (Romans 8:16) John R. Rice remarked, "I believe in heart-felt religion, and thank God for the joy He gives day by day. However, nowhere in the Bible can we find information on how one must feel before he is saved or after he is saved. Feeling varies with the person saved." (Rice Xii)

Assurance of Salvation

The assurance of salvation must be based soundly upon God's Word to me, God's Work for me, and God's Witness in me.

God's Word to Me. "These things have I written unto you that believe on the name of the Son of God; that ye may know that ye have eternal life, and that ye may believe on the name of the Son of God." (I John 5:13) Unlike John's Gospel that is written to win the lost, the Epistle of First John is written to saints to assure them of eternal life based upon the promises of the Word of God. The bottom line concerning salvation is what God states regarding it in Holy Scripture. (Romans 10:9-13; John 3:16; Acts 20:21) "Man accepts the witness (word) of pharmacists regarding prescription medication, bankers regarding bank statements, and the US Treasury regarding the value of a dollar (a dollar is worth a dollar). John emphatically declares that "the witness (word) of God is greater (more sure, certain, reliable)" than that of man. (1 John 5:9) "He is the Great Physician and will heal our souls instantly if we will trust Him. As we would trust a doctor, submit to his treatment and depend on him for results, so we should trust Jesus today regarding our souls." (Rice Xiii) "The voice of sin may be loud, but the voice of forgiveness is louder." (Moody, Prevailing Prayer, 68)

God's Work for Me. Jesus died upon the Cross and was raised from the dead to make possible salvation. The moment Christ is invited into one's life His work of reconciliation and regeneration instantly takes place. The following scripture texts reveal Christ's work in the life of the sinner at the moment of salvation regarding sin: He takes them away (John 1:29); He forgets them (Hebrews 10:17); He washes them away (Isaiah 1: 17-18); He blots them out (Isaiah 43:25); He wipes them out like a cloud (Isaiah 44:22); He pardons them (Isaiah 55:7); He buries them in the depths of the sea (Micah 7:19); and He separates them from Himself as far as the east is from the west. (Psalm 103:12)

God's Witness in Me. This witness is two-fold. First note *the witness of the Holy Spirit.* At conversion, the Holy Spirit takes up residence in the heart and bears witness to the believer that he has been passed from death unto life. "The Spirit itself beareth witness with our spirit that we are the children of God." (Romans 8:16) Second is the *witness of a changed life.* Conversion results in change. (2 Corinthians 5:17) It is impossible for the 'Born Again' to remain the same in conscience, conviction and conduct. An old African-American saying makes this point, "The day I got saved, my feet got a brand new walk, and my speech got a brand new talk." A difference occurs at salvation that continues to progress throughout the Christian's life. One of my all time gospel favorites is *It's Different Now*, a David Beatty hymn that proclaims this biblical truth.

It's different now since Jesus saved my soul
It's different now since Jesus made me whole
Ole Satan had to flee when Jesus rescued me
Now it's different oh so different now.

Vance Havner stated, "We only have one option: we can receive the Lord or reject Him. But once we receive Him, our option ends. We are no longer our own but bought with a price. We belong to Him. He has the first word and the last. He demands absolute loyalty beyond that of any earthly dictator but He has the right to do it. 'Love so amazing, so divine, demands my soul, my life, my all.' How foolish to say, "Nobody is going to tell me how much to give, what to do." We have already been told! We are His and His Word is final... I came to Christ as a country boy. I did not unders-tand all about the plan of salvation. One does not have to understand it, he has only to stand on it. But one thing I did understand even as a lad: I understood that I was under new management. I belonged to Christ and He was Lord." (Havner 117- 118) The Lordship of Christ testifies to the fact of the reality of personal salvation.

Assurance of salvation, then, is to be based upon God's Word to me, God's Work for me, and God's Witness in me. God's Word makes the believer *sure,* God's Work makes the believer *safe,* and God's Witness makes the believer *secure.* Satan "tells us most assuredly we cannot be saved. Remember, sinner, it is not *thy hold* of Christ that saves thee – it is Christ; it is not *thy joy* in Christ that saves thee – it is Christ; it is not even faith in Christ, though that is the instrument – it is Christ's blood and merits; therefore look not so much to thy hand with which thou art grasping Christ as to Christ; look not to thy hope, but to Christ, the source of thy hope; look not to thy faith; and if thou do that, ten thousand devils can not throw thee down, but as long as thou lookest at thyself, the meanest of those evil spirits may tread thee beneath his feet." (Spurgeon, Spurgeon's Sermons Vol 2, 309)

Never be ashamed of the decision to become a Christian. (Romans 1:16; Matthew 10:32-33) This confession of Christ, whether in solitude or a multitude, in daylight or twilight, in bliss of life or in the throes of death, will be discussed in Chapter Nine.

Write on a piece of paper YOUR STORY, how you came to the point of realizing a personal need of the New Birth and was saved. Share date, place, and circumstances wherein possible.

Make Sure Your Life Was Worth Saving

A man risked his life swimming through dangerous rip tides to rescue a young man. Catching his breath, the boy said to his rescuer, "Thank you for saving me." The man responded, "That's okay kid. Just make sure your life was worth saving." May all the ransomed of God who were rescued from the rip tides of eternal condemnation by Jesus "make sure their life was worth saving."

Vocational Christian Service

God is still in the business of calling His people into vocational ministry. A shortage of missionaries, pastors, evangelists, children and youth ministers, and musicians and music leaders is certainly not due to few being called out by God but rather to either an ignorance about its possibility or an unwillingness to hear or hearken to it. God will call clearly and unmistakably, taking steps to insure the right man receives the right call. He called Jonah by name, mentioned his father's name, and even cited the place where they lived. (Jonah 1:1) God removed from Jonah's mind any doubt about the validity or specificity of the call. (Jonah 1:2) He does so for everyone whom He extends such a call.

Concerning God's question in Isaiah 6:8, "Whom shall I send? And who will go for me?" John Wesley wrote George Whitfield asking, "What, Mr. Whitefield, if thou art that man?" (South in Building 131) Whitefield shook a continent for God. Each Christian is asked that same question: "What if thou art that man?" What if God is calling to missions, the pastorate, evangelism, student ministry, or music ministry? Each Christian should stand ready to respond with Isaiah, Whitefield, and millions of others, "Here am I. Send me, send me." Hudson Taylor, missionary to China, said "All giants have been weak men and women who did great things for God because they reckoned on His power and presence to be with them." (Zuck 169) C.H. Spurgeon stated, "The call of Christ's servants comes from above. Jesus stands on the mountain, evermore above the world in holiness, earnestness, love and power. Those whom he calls must go up the mountain to him, they must seek to rise to his level by living in constant communion with him. They may not be able to mount to classic honors, or attain scholastic eminence, but they must like Moses go up into the mount of God and have familiar intercourse with the unseen God, or they will never be fitted to proclaim the gospel of peace." (Spurgeon, Morning, September 10)

Sincerely, earnestly, intently, passionately say with the songwriter,

> When He calls me I will answer,
> When He calls me I will answer,
> When He calls me I will answer,
> I'll be somewhere listening for my name.

I will never forget the time nor place that God called me, a 16-year-old, into vocational Christian service. What an honor and privilege to be "called out" by God for vocational ministry. Indeed, as another has said, "If God calls you into the ministry, don't stoop to be a President or a King." William Booth stated, "Do not stop to enquire about your ability or worthiness to perform the task. All you want to know about it is 'Is it my duty?'" (Booth "Duty") The Church at large is to pray for an increase of full-time servants. "The harvest truly *is* plenteous, but the labourers *are* few; pray ye therefore the Lord of the harvest, that he will send forth labourers into his harvest." (Matthew 9:37-38) The call to vocational Christian ministry is for life or until Christ withdraws it regardless of its cost or consequence.

Digging Deeper
1. How do you know that you are a Christian?
2. What role do feelings play in salvation?
3. List eight things that happen to sin at the moment of salvation?
4. What are the two conditions of salvation?

5. What false security did you have to climb over to experience real salvation? How can you help others to move beyond the same to true faith in Jesus Christ?
6. How can one know if God is calling them into vocational Christian work?

3

CHURCH

"I believe that every Christian ought to be joined to some visible church; that is his plain duty, according to the Scriptures. God's people are not dogs, else they might go about one by one; but they are sheep, and therefore they should be in flocks." C.H. Spurgeon (servantsheatfellowship.com)

Scripture exhorts the Christian not to neglect corporate worship with other believers. (Hebrews 10:25) The Greek word for church is *ekklesia,* which comes from the Greek verb *kaleo ("to call")* and the preposition *ek* ("out"), "The called out ones." *Ekklesia* also may be translated to mean "assembly" because it was a word used to describe a people who were "called out to a meeting." The word church is found 115 times in the New Testament; 92 times it means the local congregation. The church is not brick and mortar but people of common faith who have been saved and called out to worship and serve God. (Colossians 1:13) Every believer needs the encouragement, instruction, correction, guidance, training and support that the church affords through the "Born Again" ones of which this "Bride of Christ" consists. Billy Graham remarked, "The Church has a very specific assignment, and only the church provides the nurture for spiritual growth." (Drummond 172) D.L. Moody said, "Church attendance is as vital to a disciple as a transfusion of rich, healthy blood to a sick man." (Moody <thinkexist>)

CHURCH MEMBERSHIP

What Church should a believer join? Regarding the church, what looks the same may not be the same. Not all churches are Biblical in belief and practice. Search out a church that unapologetically preaches and practices the whole teaching of the Bible, as well as one that is mission minded and evangelistic. Look for a church that proclaims the deity of Jesus Christ; His virgin birth, virtuous life, vicarious death, victorious resurrection, verifiable ascension, and visible return to earth one day. Look for a church that welcomes "the good, the bad, and the ugly" spiritually and physically. Look for a church that views herself as a hospital for sinners and not a museum for saints. A hospital is a place for caring people to take care of sick people, not condoning sickness but endeavoring to heal it. The New Testament church as a spiritual hospital is to render love, forgiveness, and care to the sin-sick compassionately without exception. However, the New Testament Church, while embracing all people in love, never sanctions or condones acts of sin they commit. The Church seeks to "reprove them" that they may become spiritually whole. Unite with a church that is not satisfied with the "status quo" of its ministry and membership but one that has an enthusiastic and challenging vision for the future. (Proverbs 29:18) Join a church that has a good "feeding trough," where the pastor and Sunday School teachers continuously serve spiritually nourishing, fortifying and challenging meals. The words of the poet John Milton sadly are true in too many congregations, "The hungry sheep look up and are not fed." (Simmonds 7) It is always wise to secure a copy of the church's constitution and covenant to review before making a decision about membership.

"A New Testament church of the Lord Jesus Christ is an autonomous local congregation of baptized believers, associated by covenant in the faith and fellowship of the gospel; observing the two ordinances of Christ, governed by His laws, exercising the gifts, rights, and privileges invested in them by His Word, and seeking to extend the gospel to the ends of the earth. Each congregation operates under the Lordship of Christ through democratic processes. In such a congregation each member is responsible and accountable to Christ as Lord. Its scriptural officers are pastors and deacons. While both men and women are gifted for service in the church, the office of pastor is limited to men as qualified by Scripture. The New Testament speaks also of the church as the Body of Christ which includes all of the redeemed of all the ages, believers from every tribe, and tongue, and people, and nation." (Baptist Faith and Message 2000)

WHY GO TO CHURCH

Go to Grow. Faithfully attend the church. (Hebrews 10:25) Attend not only its worship services but its Sunday School in order to grow and abound in the things of God. Jesus loved the church so much He died for it. May the saint at least love the church enough to show up when its doors of worship and study are opened. (Ephesians 5:25) No campus ministry or television evangelist or pastor broadcast can substitute for the Christian's involvement in the local church. C.H. Spurgeon remarked, "Now, I know there are some who say, "Well, I hope I have given myself to the Lord, but I do not intend to give myself to any church, because—" Now, why not? "Because I can be a Christian without it." Now, are you quite clear upon that? You can be as good a Christian by disobedience to your Lord's commands as by

being obedient? I do not believe it, Sir! nor do you either."
(C.H. Spurgeon, "Joining the Church," Sermon #3411)

Go to Show. Affiliation with and dedication to a local church is a witness to the world of the believer's allegiance to Jesus Christ. (Matthew 16:18)

Go to Know. In the church believers are aligned with people who love Jesus and "spur" each other onward in the Christian journey both in word and example. (Acts 2:42) The gigantic Redwoods, which have shallow root systems, withstand the force of mighty storms by intertwining their roots with each other. Young believers especially have shallow roots spiritually and will surely falter amidst Satanic assault unless their roots are intertwined with mature believers in the church. "Some people think of their spiritual life as if they were one person in a telephone booth, talking to God on a private line. They don't want to be bothered by the demands of 'organized religion' and don't think they need anyone else. 'Oh yeah, I'm spiritual they say, "I just don't like church." To those folks I say: You cannot grow spiritually in isolation." (DeVos 456)

Go to Bestow. David declared, "But as for me, I will come *into* thy house in the multitude of thy mercy: *and* in thy fear will I worship toward thy holy temple." (Psalm 5:7) "Praise ye the LORD. Sing unto the LORD a new song, *and* his praise in the congregation of saints." (Psalm 149:1) and "Make a joyful noise unto the LORD, all ye lands. Serve the LORD with gladness: come before his presence with singing. Know ye that the LORD he *is* God: *it is* he *that* hath made us, and not we ourselves; *we are* his people, and the sheep of his pasture. Enter into his gates with thanksgiving, *and* into his courts with praise: be thankful unto him, *and* bless his name." (Psalm 100: 1-4) A primary purpose in attendance at church is to engage in the corporate worship of God, offering unto Him the sacrifice of praise and thanksgiving with the lips of adoration. "To worship God is to ascribe to Him the worth of which He is worthy." (<u>Evangelical Dictionary</u>) Worship is responding to God's graciousness, goodness and being. Worship must not be designated or confined for Sunday at church. The believer is to worship God with lip and life (externally and internally) continuously both in and outside the church by living a life focused and oriented to His purpose and pleasure. Jerry Bridges stated, "Both private and corporate worship – that which we do individually and that which we do with other believers – are taught in Scripture, and the vitality and genuineness of corporate worship are to a large degree dependent upon the vitality of our individual private worship." (Bridges 16)

Go to Sow. The church is a place of service. (Ephesians 2:10; Matthew 28: 18 -20) A person is not saved to sit down and sit but to get up and get! In and through the varied evangelistic and missionary ministries of the church, the believer is able to make a difference for eternity in the lives of others locally and even globally by giving financially, witnessing, praying and serving in various capacities. A soldier strayed from his troop and finally joined the ranks of another army regiment. Immediately he asked an officer, "What can I do?" "Fall in anywhere," the officer replied, "there's good fighting all along the line." Good advice for the new believer with regard to service in the church. "Fall in anywhere for within and without the walls of the church there is plenty ministry to do." Commenting on I Samuel 13:20, the British pastor C.H. Spurgeon stated, "We are engaged in a great war with the Philistines of evil. Every weapon within our reach must be used. Preaching, teaching, praying, giving, all must be brought into action, and talents which have been thought too mean for service, must now be employed. Each moment of time, in season or out of season; each fragment of ability, educated or untutored; each opportunity, favorable or unfavorable, must be used, for our foes are many and our force but slender." (Spurgeon, <u>Morning</u>, March 2) When a person is lacking a "want to" to work, what is sometimes needed is an assignment to fuel a desire to serve. Volunteer!

Go to Glow. A growing Christian is a glowing Christian. A glowing believer radiates the likeness of Christ in word and deed (Matthew 5:14-16). He is a believer of whom others "take knowledge that they have been with Jesus" (Acts 4:13); testify regarding "Sir, we see Jesus." (John 12:21) and "I perceive that this day a holy man of God, who passeth by us continually." (2 Kings 4:9) The ministry of the church enables the Christian to be "examples to all that believe" (1 Thessalonians 1:7) and penetrating lights to those in spiritual darkness. (Luke 11:36; Proverbs 4:18; Isaiah 42:6)

SPIRITUAL OFFICES IN THE CHURCH

The Office of Pastor (Ephesians 4:11; I Peter 5: 2-4)

The primary role of the teaching pastor is to feed, equip (train), protect, and shepherd the flock of God. Regarding the pastor, W.A. Criswell stated, "In the New Testament sense, there are three words to describe the office of your preacher: *episkopos, presbuteros,* and *poimen. Episkopos* is translated 'bishop' in our language; *presbuteros* is translated 'elder;' and *poimen* is translated 'pastor.' And here in the New Testament, all three of those words refer to the same office, to the same man. He's a bishop; he's an elder; he's a pastor." (Criswell "St. Patrick") The pastor serves as the "shepherd" of the church as ordained and sanctioned by God. The Apostle Paul says regarding the pastor, "And we beseech you, brethren, to know them which labor among you, and are over you in the Lord, and admonish you; And to esteem them very highly in love for their work's sake." (I Thessalonians 5: 12-13) Pastors are God's representatives to His people who perform His work; therefore, they must be held in high regard and love. This esteem is not to be based on personality or charm but upon the fact the pastor is God's anointed man filling a divinely appointed place. Paul further states that members within the body must submit to pastoral authority so that "peace" prevails within the church. (v 14) All pastors are to be honored but some are "worthy of double honor". (I Timothy 5:17) C.H. Spurgeon, commenting on the need for more pastors, remarked, "I do not mean that we lack muffs, who occupy the pulpits and empty the pews. I believe the market has for many years been sufficiently supplied therewith; but we lack men who can stir the heart, arouse the conscience, and build up the church. The scatterers of flocks may be found everywhere; the gatherers of them, how many have we of such? Such a man at this day is more precious than the gold of Ophir." (Spurgeon "Ascension") Qualifications for a pastor are set forth in I Timothy 3:1-7. C.H. Spurgeon remarked, "Faithful preachers are among God's best gifts. Cherish them, and be obedient to their admonitions. I have known persons become offended when a minister is "too personal;" but wise men always prize a ministry in proportion as it is personal to themselves. He who never tells me of my faults, nor makes me feel uneasy, is not likely to be the means of good to my soul. What is the use of a dog that never barks?" (Spurgeon "Ascension")

"The picture of the shepherd is indelibly written on the New Testament. He was the man who cared for the flock and led the sheep into safe places; he was the man who sought the sheep when they wandered away and, if need be, died to save them. The shepherd of the flock of God is the man who bears God's people on his heart, who feeds them with the truth, who seeks them when they stray away, and who defends them from all that would hurt their faith." William Barclay (<u>Daily Study</u> 148)

Deacon (I Timothy 3: 8 – 13; Acts 6: 1-7)

The role of the deacon is to assist the pastor in spiritual and temporal matters to grant him quality time in prayer and the ministry of the Word. (Acts 6:4) Note the order of importance cited in this text for the pastor. It is prayer first, then preaching. The term *deacon* comes from the Greek word *diakonos* ("servant" or "minister"). Its meaning includes in the whole of scripture: "caring for those in prison (Matthew 25:44), serving tables (meeting physical needs, Acts 6:2), teaching the Word of God (Acts 6:4), giving money to meet others' needs (2 Corinthians 9:1), and all service offered by Christians to others to build them up in faith (1 Corinthians 12:5; Ephesians 4:12)." (Expository Dictionary 60-62) The deacon nowhere in scripture is given authority over the pastor or power to "rule" the church. Qualifications for a deacon are set forth in I Timothy 3: 8-13.

The Office of Evangelist in the Church at Large

Christ instituted the office of evangelist at the same time He did that of the pastoral office. (Ephesians 4:11) It is startling and heart-rending that Christians in many churches do not have any idea of the specific call and function of the evangelist within the body of Christ. In fact, if a hundred Christians were asked about the office or role of the vocational evangelist there would be a hundred different answers. It is time for believers to engage in a Biblical study of the vocational Evangelist to expose erroneous assumptions and embrace Jesus' view and assigned role regarding them. (Ephesians 4:11-12) The misunderstanding and neglect of the office of *pastor* by Christians would undermine God's purpose for the church; likewise does the ignorance or blatant neglect of that of the work of the *evangelist*. Billy Graham, commenting on the confusion that exists concerning the work of the evangelist, said, "And yet we cannot risk confusion if we are to make the impact on our generation that God expects of us." (Douglas 5) The evangelist is clearly as distinct a gift to the church by Christ as that of the pastor. Regarding the office of pastor and evangelist, C.H. Spurgeon commented, "If the ministry should become weak and feeble among us, the church richly deserves it, for this, the most important part of her whole organization, has been more neglected than anything else." (Spurgeon "Ascension") The word *evangelist* means to announce the Good News, to proclaim the gospel of Christ. An evangelist is a traveling preacher who is divinely set aside and gifted by God to proclaim the message of the Cross to the unsaved. "Evangelists are a gift of Christ to the churches and are not to be despised, rejected, neglected, or unjustly criticized. Their work is just as important in its relationship to the whole program of Christ as the work of other gifts mentioned..." (Whitsell 117)

Pastors and evangelists support the work of each other. Primarily, evangelists are *obstetricians* and pastors are *pediatricians.* (Steadman "Church's Building") Evangelists are harvest men given to the church. They are gifted in the spiritual birthing of the unsaved while pastors nurture the new born edifying the body of Christ. (1 Corinthians 3:4–9) Wayne Barber stated, "So you have your evangelists, then you have your pastor/teachers. These are the Master's men. Instead of gifts bestowed upon men, we have got gifted men bestowed upon the church. This is so the church can begin to grow and come into the stature of the fullness of Christ. It is required to be equipped, so He gives the equippers to the church." (Barber) C.H. Spurgeon remarked, "There remain rich gifts among us still, which I fear we do not sufficiently prize. Among men God's richest gifts are men of high vocation, separated for the ministry of the gospel. From our ascended Lord come all true *evangelists;* these are they who preach the gospel in divers places, and find it the power of God unto salvation; they are founders of churches, breakers of new soil, men of a missionary spirit, who build not on other men's foundations, but dig out for themselves. We need many such deliverers of the good news where as yet the message has not been heard. I scarcely know of any greater blessing to the church than the sending forth of earnest, indefatigable, anointed men of God, taught of the Lord to be winners of souls." (Spurgeon "Ascension")

The biblical evangelist is set apart by Christ for the building up of the church numerically. One serves in this capacity not because he is second rate, unable to "make it as a pastor," but because it is a divine call. Unlike that of the pastoral office, the evangelist ministry is not restricted to one church but to the church of Christ at large. The evangelist's livelihood (means of financial support) is dissimilar to that of a pastor and is to be provided by the churches, camps, and conferences he serves and Christians at large. The evangelist lives and serves by faith in a full time capacity believing God through His people to sustain both his family and ministry. "The only non-salaried full-time workers in the Southern Baptist Convention are evangelists." (Fordham, Personal Correspondence) The evangelist lives an uncommon life. He moves about constantly from city to city, is *often* separated from family and friends, sleeps in various places at various times, eats irregularly, lives with uncertainty about how bills and living needs will be supplied, and serves people who at times are critical, yet he is all the while excited and grateful to do what he does for Christ. Pray that "the Lord of the harvest" will raise up more evangelists, that He will open "doors of utterance" for the evangelist, and that the needs of the evangelist will be supplied "according to the riches of God in Christ Jesus."

A picture of the Biblical Evangelist is Phillip. (Acts 21:8; 8: 26-40) The *motive* of the evangelist is the divine call placed upon his life. (8:26; Ephesians 4:11) The evangelist has no discretionary power to alter this call; he must simply obey it. He is one *thrust* into the work of evangelism by the

Holy Spirit and is passionate about doing it. The *message* of the evangelist is "Jesus Christ and Him crucified". (8: 35) Prior to a Crusade in Osaka, Japan, the Governor of Osaka asked Billy Graham, "Why is it that the church in Japan is about the same as it was in the 17th century?" Answering his own question he said, "I believe it is because the Gospel has not been made clear to the Japanese people. I hope that you will make it clear." (Douglas 7) The evangelist's task is to make the presentation of the gospel crystal clear in America and regions beyond so all can understand. The *method* of the evangelist is simply readiness *to go* and *tell* the gospel story to all people regardless of place, people, or price compassionately. (8:27, 40) The evangelist knows how to present Christ to the unsaved tactfully but also is gifted by God to draw the net bringing the lost to a decision whether privately or in public services. (8:37) "In the Southern Baptist Convention, revival meetings are the number one way evangelists are used. In fact, in 1986, one-third of all the people saved in Southern Baptist Convention churches were saved during the six weeks of simultaneous revivals, according to Richard Harris of the Home Mission Board." (Fordham, The Evangelist, 7) With revival meetings in decline, the church must utilize the evangelist for other ministries and embrace him financially. Failure to do so, I fear, will eventually force gifted evangelists out of the ministry. Churches at large and Christians in general should consider supporting an evangelist financially and prayerfully. (Matthew 10:10)

Myths about the Biblical Evangelist
1. He is a pastor like the pastor of the host church sponsoring the revival.
2. The State or National Convention or another church pays the evangelist a salary.
3. The evangelist is in evangelism because of failure in the pastorate or other ministry.
4. All evangelists are of the same temperament and giftedness.
5. The work of the evangelist is not divinely ordained or authorized as that of the pastor.
6. The work of the evangelist has ceased and his office rescinded by God.

The *office of evangelist* was established by our ascending Lord to plant churches, partner with churches in evangelism, pursue souls, preach the Gospel and perfect ("equip") the saint. This office has not been deleted and the evangelist's call has not been rescinded by Christ. It will not "Till we all come in the unity of the faith, and of the knowledge of the Son of God, unto a perfect man, unto the measure of the stature of the fullness of Christ." (Ephesians 4:13) Its recognition and utilization is needed more now than ever. Evangelist Don Womack preaching on the subject of "Ethics in Evangelism" stated, "It is a sin of commission to reject the divine office of the evangelist: a sin of omission to ignore the office; and a sin of transgression to abuse the office." (Trent 14) Billy Graham stated, "The calling of evangelist is one of the great gifts that God has given to the church, and is as important as the seminary professor, or church pastor...A great need in the church today is to recognize and dignify the gift of the evangelist." (Adler 43) Faris Whitsell said, "We conclude, then, that Christ still grants the evangelistic gift to chosen men. Churches should recognize and use evangelists. If so –called evangelists have been unworthy of the title, that does not mean that evangelists as a class have been discredited." (Whitsell 123)

The office of Apostle has ceased since obviously it is impossible for anyone to meet the qualifications set forth in Acts 1:21-22. *The office of Prophet* as it relates to foretelling events, as with Agabus regarding a famine (Acts 11:28) and Paul's arrest in Jerusalem (Acts 21:10-11), has likewise ceased. "Because the foundation of the church has been laid and the canon of Scripture is complete, there is no need for the gift of prophecy." (Enns 271) Paul teaches that both the office of apostle and prophet were ordained by God expressly for the foundation stage of the church. (Ephesians 2:20) John MacArthur espoused that these two offices were replaced by the office of evangelists and teaching pastors. (MacArthur, Study Bible, Ephesians 4:11)

MENTORING

Paul instructs older women in the church to mentor the young women in regard to seven matters. (Titus 2: 2 – 5) The older men in the church have an equal responsibility to mentor the young men. Barnabas took Paul, while just a babe in Christ, under his wings and developed him in the things of Christ. Luke writes, "But Barnabas took him (Paul) and brought him to the apostles, and declared unto them how he had seen the Lord in the way, and that he had spoken to him, and how he had preached boldly at Damascus in the name of Jesus." (Acts 9:27) The words "took him" literally mean that Barnabas physically held on to Paul to help him. The Apostle Paul would not have become what he was for God had it not been for Barnabas' mentorship in his early life. The failure of the spiritually mature to coach growing believers, church leaders and preacher-boys is the great weakness of the modern church movement. I firmly believe that the ministry of mentoring (spiritually coaching) is the greatest work that can be done outside of soul winning.

Mentoring is the ministry of taking younger men or women under one's protective and provisional wings to edify, educate, embolden, emancipate, enlighten, establish, excite, and equip in spiritual matters. This work, though joyful, is extremely demanding and occasionally disappointing. It requires time, resources, sacrifice, devotion and prayers. Robert E. Coleman commented, "What perhaps is the most difficult part of the whole process of training is that we must anticipate their problems and prepare them for what they will face. This is terribly hard to do and can become exasperating. It means that we can seldom put them out of our mind. Even when we are in our private meditations and study, our disciples will be in our prayers and dreams. Would a parent who loves his children want it any other way? We have to accept the burden of their immaturity until such time as they can do it for themselves." (Coleman 123-124)

An excellent pattern for mentoring (coaching) is found in that of the Apostle Paul to Timothy. (2 Timothy 1 – 3)

It involves *Conviction*. (1:11) The blind cannot lead the blind; thus, it is imperative the mentor be a person of biblical soundness, separation and surrender. It involves *Confirmation*. (1: 5-6) The infusion of confidence and certainty regarding salvation (and) or one's ministry call by the mentor is essential. The coach has to help the disciple believe in himself. It involves *Cultivation*. (1:13; 3:14) This requires imparting God's Word to the soul and watering until it sprouts. The mentor must constantly sow sound biblical doctrine and teaching into the disciple. The spiritual coach must be as a "Barking Dog" to the disciple, continuously warning of potential "snares," heresy, and soul neglect. It involves *Correction*. (1:7) The mentor must confront moral and spiritual faults and weaknesses. (Galatians 6:1) He holds the disciple accountable morally, ethically and spiritually. It involves *Commendation*. (1:3) The display of approval in lessons learned and battles won encourages the disciple to press forward. Imagine how Timothy's heart must have raced in hearing that a spiritual giant like Paul thanked God for him and believed in him. Render praise when praise is due. It involves *Clarification*. (2: 16-19)The mentor's task is to clear up any misunderstanding or misinterpretation regarding scripture or decision made. It involves *Compulsion*. (1:14; 2:3; 2:22; 3:14; 4:1-5) The spiritual coach must compel, incite, and motivate the disciple to keep a tight grip upon "that good thing (Gospel) which was committed unto them by the Holy Ghost." (1:14) The disciple must be taught patience, persistence, and to see his potential despite suffering, persecution, failure, or discouragement. He must be exhorted never to quit or give up on the faith or divine call.

Solomon said, "Iron sharpeneth iron." (Proverbs 27:17) The Lord is counting on the spiritually mature to sharpen the iron of young believers doctrinally, devotionally and dutifully until they then can do the same for another. Young Christians or those going into any ministry should seek out a godly person to be a coach in spiritual things (always of the same sex). The spiritually mature must now, more than ever, invest in new believers and young ministers, allowing the mighty rivers of their spiritual knowledge and experience to flow into them and then through them.

In response to the question, "If you were a pastor of a large church in a principal city, what would be your plan of action?" Billy Graham replied, "I think one of the first things I would do would be to get a small group of eight, or ten, or twelve men around me that would meet a few hours a week and pay the price! It would cost them something in time and effort. I would share everything I have, over a period of years. Then I would actually have twelve ministers among the laymen who in turn could take eight or ten or twelve more and teach them. ...Christ, I think, set the pattern. He spent most of His time with twelve men. He didn't spend it with the great crowd. In fact, every time He had a great crowd it seems to me that there weren't too many results. The great results, it seems to me, came in his personal interview and in the time He spent with His twelve." (Coleman 119-120)

The mentored disciple, certainly in time, will declare to his spiritual coach the words of Laban to Jacob, "*For* I have learned by experience that the LORD hath blessed me for thy sake." (Genesis 30:27)

The 'How To' concerning Church Membership

When a believer asked a friend during the sermon invitation, "Are you ready to join the church?" the friend replied, "I don't know how." How is one to unite with the church? At the conclusion of a church worship service, an invitation to respond to the message preached will be extended. It is at this point a person may approach the pastor indicating the desire to unite with the church. Some churches provide additional ways to join their fellowship.

The Invitation

The invitation at the climax of a sermon is customary in most of our churches. Some question its purpose and criticize its practice. Some see it merely as an addendum to the sermon, a time to prepare to exit the sanctuary. I see it as a vital part of the sermon. Billy Graham, speaking to evangelists from around the world at Amsterdam '83, said, "Is it valid or legitimate to extend an invitation for people to come to Christ?" Then he answered this question with an emphatic, "Yes!". (Douglas 171)

In stressing the importance of the invitation, C.E. Matthews declared, "When the service is concluded and the congregation stands for the invitation, the moment has struck for the consummation of everything that has been done in the name of the Lord up to that hour for that one thing. All the work in preparation - the census, the contacts in visitation, the publicity, the prayer meetings, money contributed, everything – was for that invitation. All that has transpired in that particular service – the sermon, the praying, the music, the time spent by the congregation in worship – everything has been done to make ready for that invitation." (Matthews 92-93)

Throughout scripture, one discovers invitation after invitation extended. God extended the first invitation to Adam and Eve after their sin when he cried out to them "Where art thou?" (Genesis 3:9) Moses issued an invitation at the base of Sinai following his sermon to the multitude of people, "Who is on the Lord's side, let him come unto me." (Exodus 32:26) Joshua issued an invitation to the Israelites in stating, "Choose you this day whom you will serve." (Joshua 24:15) Jesus extended the invitation to Simon and Andrew when He said, "Come ye after me, and I will make you to become fishers of men." (Mark 1:17) Jesus issued a clear invitation in Revelation 3:20, "Behold I stand at the door and knock if any man hear my voice and open the door I will come to him."

Primarily due to lack of instruction, many church members are clueless about their responsibility in the invitation. In speaking on this subject at a conference the response from Christians was "I never heard a sermon on the invitation until tonight." C.E. Matthews shared the confession of a church member who, after hearing a talk about the invitation, stated, "Pastor, I never realized how I had failed in my responsibility when an invitation was given in the service. I have just been awakened to a thing that I have never known before, and that is the tremendous burden that must be on the heart of a preacher when he is making his appeal and trying to persuade people to accept Christ as Savior. I am ashamed of myself. When you begin the invitation, I have been guilty of powdering my face and applying lipstick without any thought of what I was doing. I have asked God to forgive me, and I am asking you to forgive me and to pray for me that I will share with you and others the responsibility of helping people decide for Christ during the invitation." (Matthews 95) Tragically, many church members unlike this lady yet understand their awesome part in the all important invitation.

The Christian's Role in the Invitation

The invitation is a time for Reflection. It is a time for reflection upon the word of God spoken and the challenges presented. "What am I being asked to do?" The invitation is a time for Inspection. "Is this something I need to do?" The invitation is a time for Deliberation. Serious consideration is to be given to the action, commitment that one needs to make. "Is this something I am willing to do?" The invitation is a time for Resolution. "Will I make this commitment here and now?" The invitation is a time for Application. Reflection, Inspection, Deliberation and Resolution lead to decision. "I will do it." It is at this point a public commitment revealing such a desire is made by the person walking the aisle to the pastor. The invitation is a time for intercession. Believers ought to pray for the unsaved to respond once personal decisions are settled.

Giving an invitational appeal at the conclusion of his sermon entitled "John 3:16," Billy Graham said, "I ask no one leave. This is the real moment for which we are here." (Lorentzen)

The serious nature of the invitation requires an attitude of reverence, receptivity and response. Distractions such as departure, talking or readying to leave the service while the invitation is in progress must be avoided. My book The Evangelistic Invitation 101 addresses this subject in depth.

Digging Deeper

1. What is the New Testament Church?
2. Is it necessary for a Christian to join a church?
3. What are the six reasons cited for a Christian going to church?
4. Why cannot Para church organizations and religious broadcasts substitute for the believer's involvement in the local church?
5. Who is eligible to join a New Testament Church?
6. How can you assist the Church in fulfilling its place in God's plan?
7. What are the roles of the pastor and deacon in the church?
8. In what ways is the evangelist a gift to the church by the ascended Lord?
9. How might the church utilize and support the evangelist?
10. Explain the role of the mentor (spiritual coach).
11. What is your role during the sermon's invitation?

4

PRAYER, FASTING AND SOLITUDE

"Why do we grow so little? Why do we win so few? Why are we weak and powerless? Because we pray so little." John Bisagno (Bisagno, Preface <u>Positive Praying</u>)

"Let's move from theology to kneeology! Power for victory in spiritual warfare is found in prayer." Robert R. Lawrence (Lawrence 634)

"The first thought and the first word of the day belong to God." Dietrich Bonhoeffer (De Gruchy 256)

"The way we end today can clearly affect the way we encounter tomorrow." C.J. Mahaney (Mahaney)

Prayer simply is talking to God. Matthew Henry remarked, "The Bible is a letter God has sent to us; prayer is a letter we send to Him." (Henry, <u>Miscellaneous Works</u> 433) Prayer is to the believer's victory over sin and fellowship with God what oxygen is to the lungs. It is absolutely vital. The discipline of prayer at the start of the day and throughout the day is essential to growth. Prayer leads to the Presence of God, the Power of God, and the Plan of God. Robert M. M'Cheyne, a Scottish preacher, declared, "I ought to spend the best hours in communion with God. It is my noblest and most fruitful employment and is not to be thrust into the corner." (Bonar 178) "It is far better," M'Cheyne said, "to begin with God - to see His face first, to get my soul near Him before it is near another." (Bounds, Purpose in Prayer, 29) A.W. Tozer wrote, "It is well that we accept the hard truth now: The man who would know God must give time to Him. He must count no time wasted that is spent in the cultivation of His acquaintance. He must give himself to meditation and prayer hours on end. So did the saints of old, the glorious company of the apostles, the Godly fellowship of the prophets and the believing members of the holy church in all generations. And so must we if we would follow in their train." (Tozer)

E.M. Bounds declared, "A desire for God that cannot break the chains of sleep is weak, able to do little for God after it has indulged itself fully. The desire for God that lags behind the Devil and the world at the beginning of the day will never catch up. The desire for God awoke the great saints of God and called them to communion with their Lord. Heeding and acting on this call gave their faith a grasp on God and gave to their hearts the sweetest and fullest revelation of God." (Bounds 491)

HOW TO PRAY

C.H. Spurgeon stated, "For real business at the mercy seat give me a home-made prayer, a prayer that comes out of the depths of your heart, not because you invented it, but because the Holy Spirit put it there. Though your words are broken and your sentences disconnected God will hear you. Perhaps you can pray better without words than with them. There are prayers that break the back of words; they are too heavy for any human language to carry." (Moody, <u>Pleasures</u>, 94) J. Wilbur Chapman remarked, "Did you ever cultivate the habit of talking aloud to God? Sit down this very day and with upturned face and open eyes talk to Him as to your father, as to the dearest friend you have, one to whom you can tell your most secret thoughts; tell them to Him. The very room where you sit will seem to be filled with angels; but best of all God will be there, for one could not long talk to Him without feeling Him to be near." (Chapman 108)

> "Let your thoughts be psalms, your prayers incense, and your breath praise." C.H. Spurgeon (Spurgeon, <u>Sermons of Rev. C.H. Spurgeon</u>, 357)

Prayer involves "asking" God. (Matthew 7:8) "Asking" works because it's the authorized and anointed means given to Christians by God to have needs met personally and for others corporately. (Matthew 7:7-8) Simply, "asking" works because God promises "Call unto me, and I will answer thee, and show thee great and mighty things, which thou knowest not." (Jeremiah 33:3) The Christian is to trust the promise of God about prayer and thus while praying exhibit faith in His ability and power to answer in accordance with His divine will and good pleasure. (James 1:6; Luke 22:42) "Answered prayer is not a miracle, it is a law. It will always be, when the laws are kept and certain rules are observed. It is always to be expected! When the child of God prays and his prayers are answered, three things have happened: he has prayed in faith believing, he has prayed specifically and has thereby met the conditions of a loving Heavenly Father, and the Father has responded." (Bisagno 10)

John Stott stated, "We need to win the battle of the prayer threshold. To help me persevere in prayer, I sometimes imagine a very high stone wall, with the living God on the other side of it. In this walled garden He is waiting for me to come to Him. There is only one way into the garden – a tiny door. Outside that door stands the devil with a drawn sword, ready to stop me. It is at this point that we need to defeat the devil in the name of Christ. That is the battle of the threshold." (Stott, <u>Maintaining</u>, 32) E.M. Bounds wrote, "We can curtail our praying and not realize the peril until the foundations are gone. Hurried devotion makes weak faith, feeble convictions, questionable piety. To be little with God is to do little for God." (Bounds, <u>Power</u>, 123) C.H. Spurgeon stated, "All hell is vanquished when the believer bows his knee in importunate supplication. Beloved brethren, let us pray. We cannot all argue, but we can all pray; we cannot all be leaders, but we can all be pleaders; we cannot all be mighty in rhetoric, but we can all be prevalent in prayer. I would sooner see you eloquent with God than with men. Prayer links us with the Eternal, the Omnipotent, the Infinite, and hence it is our chief resort. . . . Be sure that you are with God, and then you may be sure that God is with you." (Spurgeon, <u>An All-Round Ministry</u>, 227)

In Matthew 6: 9-13 the Lord gives believers a model prayer. This prayer is not intended to be prayed verbatim continuously but to serve as a pattern for prayer. Jon Courson states, "I can't hit like Babe Ruth, paint like Michelangelo, or sing like George Beverly Shea. But you know what? I can pray like John Knox, like Martin Luther, and like Charles Spurgeon, because I can pray the same prayer they prayed. It is the perfect prayer because it came from the perfect Pray-er: Jesus Christ. You can pray this prayer daily, hourly, whenever you like. And you will find yourself in incredible company with the great saints of the ages, with believers of all other flavors, who all love God and address Him as Father because of their relationship to the Son." (Courson, Matthew 6: 9-13)

God's Power to be remembered. "Our Father who art in Heaven." Enveloped in the word "our" is the story of man's redemption from Satan and Sin unto God. Only the "Born Again," due to their adoption into His family as 'sons and daughters,' have the privilege and honor to address God in this personal manner. (Galatians 4: 4-7; Romans 8:14-15) "But as many as received him, to them gave he power to become the sons of God, *even* to them that believe on his name: Which were born, not of blood, nor of the will of the flesh, nor of the will of man, but of God." (John 1:12) "For I am not ashamed of the gospel of Christ: for it is the power of God unto salvation to every one that believeth; to the Jew first, and also to the Greek." (Romans 1:16) Express gratitude to God for making this union possible and for granting access to His throne 24/7.

God's Person to be reverenced. "Hallowed be Thy name." You are to pray that God's name (It speaks of who God is and His holiness, love, power, authority) will be treated with respect and reverence.

God's Program to be expanded. "Thy kingdom come." You are to pray that's God's rule will encompass the whole world. Pray that there will be less and less sin and more and more people who love Jesus. Wouldn't it really be great if everybody loved Jesus and lived for Him? You are to pray for that to be true. Pray for friends and others to be saved. On a daily routine, pray, "Lord help me do my part in fulfilling the Great Commission today that your Kingdom will come sooner than later."

God's Plan to be accomplished. "Thy will be done." You are to pray that what God wants to do in, with, and through your life will be done totally without hindrance or delay just as it is done among the host of Heaven. To pray in this manner, lay aside personal wants and desires and be completely open to His plan for your life, a plan that may include vocational

Christian service. You are to pray that His will also will be fulfilled in Christians, the church, and nations.

God's Provision to be given. "Give us this day our daily bread." Pray for God to give you everything needed. In sickness ask Him to give health, in times of loneliness to give a friend, in times of hunger to give food, and in times of sorrow to comfort. There is no need to worry about tomorrow since God is as in control of it as He is of today. Just ask Him to help and He will. Andrew Murray stated, "When the child (Christian) has yielded himself to the Father in the care for His name, His Kingdom and His will, he has full liberty to ask for his daily bread." (Murray, With Christ, 34)

God's Pardon to be known. "Forgive us our debts (sins) as we forgive our debtors." In the same measure believers forgive when wronged, they are to pray God will forgive them. In the same manner God forgives the believer (without deserve) the believer is to forgive those who do him wrong. Jon Courson wrote, "When people fail, don't rub it in. Rub it out. Forgive them." (Courson, Matthew 6:14-15) D.A. Carson stated, "All of us would be wiser if we would resolve never to put people down, except on our prayer lists." (Carson) Fellowship with, not relationship to God, demands believers forgive others. Daily, confess and repent of sin. Keep short accounts of sin. Don't save spiritual soiled garments until "wash day." Wash 'em daily! (I John 1:7-9)

God's Prevention to be experienced. "And lead us not into temptation." Pray that God will not just protect from sin but from the temptation that causes it and from walking into its arena. Without temptation to do wrong, chances are you won't. The believer at the dawn of each new day should pray, "O Lord keep me from temptation today and especially the one that doth so easily beset me." (Hebrews 12:1)

God's Protection to be demonstrated. "But deliver me from the evil one." You are to pray that God will not allow Satan to harm or injure your spiritual walk. "Greater is He that is in me then he that is in the world." (I John 4:4) God is able to give the power and strength to defeat Satan.

God's Praise to be exhibited. "For thine is the Kingdom, the power and the glory forever. Amen." This model prayer ends with a doxology of praise. Praise is giving God the honor due Him. Close your prayers with telling God how much you love Him, adore Him, and revere Him. John Calvin remarked of this closing doxology, saying it "not only warms our hearts to press toward the glory of God... but also to tell us that all our prayers... have no other foundation than God alone." (Calvin 213)

PRAY USING ACTS

Use the acrostic of the word *ACTS* in praying. You may base your prayer in this sequential order.

A   adoration (praise and worship to God)
C   confession (repentance and cleansing)
T   thanksgiving (gratitude for salvation, daily provision and protection)
S   supplication (petitioning God, Matthew 7:7)

PRAY SCRIPTURE AND MEDIATIONS

There is no greater praying than that of praying scripture. Prayers that can be adapted easily and prayed personally abound in the Psalms and throughout the Bible.

Regarding David's prayer in Psalm 5:1-3, Bible commentator Matthew Henry stated, "David's prayers were not his words only, but his mediations; as mediation is the best preparative for prayer, so prayer is the best issue of mediation. Mediation and prayer should go together." (Henry, Commentary Vol. 3, 255)

PRAY THE PRAYERS OF THE SAINTS AND HYMNS

The Valley of Vision, a collection of prayers of the saints, is a tremendous aid to the believer in jump-starting personal prayers. Additionally, hymns of the faith can be personalized and turned upward to God in praise and prayer. The prayers of the saints and hymns are not to substitute for personal praying but serve as a springboard in praying heartfelt and passionate prayers.

In 1695, Thomas Ten formatted one launch pad for prayer at the start of day by declaring to God,

"Direct, control, suggest, this day,
All I design, or do, or say
That all my powers, with all their might,
In Thy sole glory may unite."

INTERCESSORY PRAYER

It is a great privilege to pray for the concerns and needs of others. Oswald Chambers declared, "The real business of your life as a saved soul is intercessory prayer." It is important to journal prayer requests. Peter Lord's *2959 Plan* is an excellent prayer plan and journal that specifies a different category of people of which to pray daily. If this guide is not available, design one as follows.

Monday: **"M"** for ministers and missionaries.
Tuesday: **"T"** for troubled people who are experiencing trials and tribulation.
Wednesday: **"W"** for workers with governing authority in the political arena.
Thursday: **"T"** for personal tasks of which God has assigned.
Friday: **"F"** for friends and foes.
Saturday: **"S"** for sinners who need salvation and saints who need revival.

Sunday: "S" for the service of the church and those who preach, sing and teach.

C.H. Spurgeon stated, "Our first prayer was a prayer for ourselves; we asked that God would have mercy upon us, and blot out our sin. He heard us. But when he had blotted out our sins like a cloud, then we had more prayers for ourselves. We have had to pray for sanctifying grace, for constraining and restraining grace; we have been led to crave for a fresh assurance of faith, for the comfortable application of the promise, for deliverance in the hour of temptation, for help in the time of duty, and for succor in the day of trial. We have been compelled to go to God for our souls, as constant beggars asking for everything. Bear witness, children of God, you have never been able to get anything for your souls elsewhere." (Spurgeon, <u>Morning</u>, February 6)

Hindrances To Prayer
Things that can hinder prayer from being effective: Disobedience (Micah 3:4; Deuteronomy 1:43-45; Jeremiah 11:10f); Arrogance (James 4:6-10; Job 35:12-13); Hypocrisy (Mark 12:38-40; Matthew 15:1-9); Refusal to help the poor (Proverbs 21:13); Un-confessed sin (John 9:31; Isaiah 59:1-2; Psalm 66:18); Unforgiving spirit; (Mark 11:25); Indifference toward the Word of God (Proverbs 28:9); Wrong relationship with husband or wife. (I Peter 3:7)

DANIEL
The prophet Daniel prayed regularly at set times and in a set place. (Daniel 6:10) Make an appointment to meet God in prayer scheduling the time and place each day. This is your "closet" prayer time. Plan the day around prayer, not prayer around the day. Praying is not to be restricted only to this time in the day because Christians are told to "Pray

continuously." (I Thessalonians 5:18; Ephesians 6:18) Prayer works, so work hard at prayer.

FASTING

Fasting is abstinence from food, amusements, relationships or television for the purpose of focusing more totally upon God. Christians do not fast and pray to change the mind of God but to give God the chance to change their mind. Christians fast to exhibit a state of mind to do what naturally they are not prone - to cut loose the instinctive nerve and impulsiveness of the flesh (carnal nature). Jesus commends the discipline of fasting, giving instruction regarding the practice. (Matthew 6:16-17) Andrew Murray remarked, "Fasting helps to express, to deepen, and to confirm the resolution that we are ready to sacrifice anything, to sacrifice ourselves to attain what we seek for the kingdom of God." (Smith, J. Harold 89) Arthur Wallis remarked, "Fasting is calculated to bring a note of urgency and importunity into our praying, and to give force to our pleading in the court of heaven. The man who prays with fasting is giving heaven notice that he is truly in earnest...Not only so, but he is expressing his earnestness in a divinely-appointed way. He is using a means that God has chosen to make his voice to be heard on high."(Whitney 164) Fasting combined with prayer and proper motive makes it acceptable unto the Lord.

Bill Bright stated, "Fasting is the most powerful spiritual discipline of all the Christian disciplines. Through fasting and prayer, the Holy Spirit can transform your life. Fasting and prayer can also work on a much grander scale. According to Scripture, personal experience and observation, I am convinced that when God's people fast with a proper Biblical motive-seeking God's face not His hand-with a broken, repentant, and contrite spirit, God will hear from heaven and heal our lives, our churches, our communities, our nation and world. Fasting and prayer can bring about revival - a change in the direction of our nation, the nations of earth and the fulfillment of the Great Commission." (Bright)

Isaiah makes plain the objective of the spiritual fast. "Is this not the purpose of the fast I have chosen? To loosen the bands of wickedness, to undo heavy burdens, and to let the oppressed go free, and that ye break every yoke?" (Isaiah 58:6) The believer is to engage in a spiritual fast to bring the body into subjection to the Spirit (I Corinthians 9:27); to prevail with God (Ezra 8:23; Mark 9:29); to liberate from the "yoke" of a sin's mastery (Isaiah 58:6 b); to give added strength in temptation (Matthew 4: 1-11); to give guidance in decision making (Nehemiah 1:4); to express mourning and repentance for personal or corporate sin (Ezra 9:5; Joel 2:12-13); to give strength to follow through victoriously with Holy Spirit led decisions (Esther 4:16); to reveal God's plan for life (Acts 10:10); to intercede for another when he/she falls into sin (I Kings 21:27); to drive Satan and the demons of Hell back (Mark 9: 17-29); to intercede for a personal enemy (Psalm 35:12-13); to humble the soul (Psalms 69:10; 1 Kings 21:27-29); to break the bondage of physical appetite (I Corinthians 6:12 -13); and to express love and devotion to God (Luke 2:37).

Various durations, from part of a day to forty days, for the fast are stated in scripture. The Lord does not impose a set timetable for the fast nor times for its observance but allows the Holy Spirit to direct the believer individually regarding both. Fasting is to be a personal and private matter not engaged to gain the attention or admiration of man but the audience of God solely. Jesus states, "Moreover when ye fast, be not, as the hypocrites, of a sad countenance: for they disfigure their faces, that they may appear unto men to fast. Verily I say unto you, they have their reward. But thou, when thou fastest, anoint thine head, and wash thy face; That thou appear not unto men to fast, but unto thy Father which is in secret: and thy Father, which seeth in secret, shall reward thee openly." (Matthew 6:16-18)

Medical council may be necessary prior to fasting. The question for the believer is not "Should I fast?" but "When should I fast, how long should I fast, and for what purpose?"

SOLITUDE

The practice of solitude is the withdrawal of one's self to a quiet and serene place in silence before the Lord. *Solitude* is "a life-giving practice that enriches our hearts with the powerful gifts of clarity, cleansing, and strength." (Warden) William Wordsworth remarked, "Solitude permits the mind to feel." (Wordsworth 508) Personally my place of solitude is at a local park in early morning where I am shut up with God to think, mediate, read, worship, and to pray inwardly. *Solitude* precedes my devotional time and together this is absolutely the best part of the day. The duration of solitude may be a few minutes to several hours or days. Jesus practiced the discipline of solitude (Luke 4:42) as did the prophet Elijah at Mount Horeb (1 Kings 19:11-13) and the Apostle Paul in Arabia (Galatians 1:17). The Lord instructs, "Be still and know that I am God." (Psalm 46:10) David declared, "Truly my soul silently waits for God; From Him comes my salvation. He only is my rock and my salvation; He is my defense; I shall not be greatly moved." (Psalm 62: 1-2, NKJV) and "My soul, wait silently for God alone, for my expectation is from Him." (Psalm 62: 5, NKJV)

Andrew Murray stated, "Let everyone who wants to learn the art of waiting on God remember the lesson: "Take heed, and be quiet"; "It is good that a man quietly wait." Take time to be separate from all friends and all duties, all cares and all joys; time to be still and quiet before God. Take time not only to secure stillness from man and the world, but from self and its energy. Let the Word and Prayer be very precious. But remember, even these may hinder the quiet waiting. The activity of the mind in studying the Word or giving expression to its thoughts in prayer, the activities of the heart, with its desires and hopes and fears, may so engage us that we do not come to the still waiting on the All-glorious One; our whole being is prostrate in silence before Him. Though at first, it may appear difficult to know how thus quietly to wait, with the activities of mind and heart for a time subdued, every effort after it will be rewarded. We will discover that it grows upon us, and the little season of silent worship will bring a peace and a rest that give a blessing not only in prayer, but all day." (Murray, Waiting, 108-109)

A.W. Tozer remarked, "Retire from the world each day to some private spot, even if it be only the bedroom (for a while I retreated to the furnace room for want of a better place). Stay in the secret place till the surrounding noises begin to fade out of your heart and a sense of God's presence envelops you…Listen for the inward Voice till you learn to recognize it. Listen to pray inwardly every moment. Call home your roving thoughts. Gaze on Christ with the eyes of your soul. Practice spiritual concentration." (Wiersbe, Best of Tozer, 151-152) "Why is it that some Christians, although they hear many sermons, make but slow advances in the divine life? Because they neglect their closets, and do not thoughtfully meditate on God's Word."(Spurgeon, Morning, October 12)

Solitude not only enriches the believer's walk with God but may lead to salvation for the unsaved. C.H. Spurgeon, in his sermon *Solitude, Silence and Submission,* stated, "I commend solitude to any of you who are seeking salvation, first, that you may *study well your case as in the sight of God.* Few men truly know themselves as they really are. Therefore, I pray you, set apart some season every day, or at least some season as often as you can get it, in which the business of your mind shall be to take your longitude and latitude, that you may know exactly where you are. You may be drifting towards the rocks, and you may be wrecked before you know your danger. I implore you, do not let your ship go at full steam through a fog; but slacken speed a bit, and heave the lead, to see whether you are in deep waters or shallow. I am not asking you to do more than any kind and wise man would advise you to do; do I even ask you more than your own conscience tells you is right? Sit alone a while, that you may carefully consider your case." (Spurgeon, "Solitude")

References on Prayer, Solitude and Fasting
With Christ in the School of Prayer, Andrew Murray
The Complete Works of E. M. Bounds On Prayer, E.M.
    Bounds
The Practice of the Presence of God, Brother Lawrence
The Autobiography of George Muller
Praying Hyde: Apostle of Prayer, Editor: Captain E.G.
    Carré
Hudson Taylor's Spiritual Secret, Hudson Taylor
Great Preaching on Prayer, Editor: Curtis Hutson
2959 Plan, Peter Lord (Park Avenue Baptist Church,
    Titusville, Florida)
The Valley of Vision, The Banner of Truth Trust
The Power of Positive Praying, John Bisagno
Only a Prayer Meeting, C.H. Spurgeon
The Pastor in Prayer (Prayers of Spurgeon), C.H. Spurgeon
Prayer: Asking and Receiving, John R. Rice
How To Spend A Day in Prayer, Lorne C. Sanny
Spiritual Disciplines of the Christian Life, Donald S.
    Whitney
Fast Your Way to Health, J. Harold Smith
Fasting For A Spiritual Breakthrough, Elmer Towns

Digging Deeper

1. What is the contrast stated between oxygen and prayer?
2. What guidance for prayer does the acrostic of the word "acts" give?
3. What lessons are gained from Daniel's prayer life?
4. What are the eight petitions of the Lord's Prayer?
5. What hinders prayer from being effective?
6. What is the purpose for the spiritual fast?
7. Share the benefits of solitude with God.

THE BIBLE

"No Spiritual Discipline is more important than the intake of God's Word. Nothing can substitute for it. There simply is no healthy Christian life apart from a diet of the milk and meat of Scripture." Donald S. Whitney (Whitney 26)

"Now the measure in which we profit from our reading and study of Scriptures may be ascertained by the extent to which Christ is becoming more real and more precious unto our hearts." A.W. Pink (Pink)

Spiritual growth depends upon the intake of God's Word. As food is vital for the body's growth, the intake of God's Word is for the soul's growth. Peter teaches that as a baby needs feeding in order to grow up into an adult, a young baby in Christ needs feeding to grow up into spiritual maturity. (I Peter 2:2) The reading and study of scripture is profitable in several ways. It is profitable in its revelation. Upon its reading, the Holy Scripture mirrors the dirt in the heart. (Psalm 119:130) Secondly, it is profitable in its sanctification in that it has a cleansing impact in its recipient. (Hebrews 4:12). Third, it is profitable in its protection. The

Psalmist declared, "Wherewithal shall a young man cleanse his way? By giving heed to the word of God." (Psalm 119:9) The Word repels sin. It has a purifying and preserving power in the life of the saint. David said, "Thy word have I hid in my heart that I may not sin against thee." (Psalm 119:11) It is profitable in its instruction "that the man of God may be perfect, thoroughly furnished ('equipped') unto all good works." (2 Timothy 3:17)

A person does not need to go outside the Bible for theological dogma or guidance about holy living. Scripture not only tells the Christian how to live but gives the wherewithal with which to live the life it espouses. (1 Corinthians 4:6) George Mueller, a Nineteenth Century pastor in England, stated, "I saw that the most important thing I had to do was give myself to the reading of the Word of God – not prayer, but the Word of God. Here again, not the simple reading of the Word of God so that it only passes through my mind just as water runs through a pipe, but considering what I read, pondering over it, and applying it to my heart. To mediate on it, that thus my heart might be comforted, encouraged, warned, reproved, instructed. And that thus, by means of the Word of God, while mediating on it, my heart be brought into experiencing Communion with the Lord." (Pierson) John MacArthur wrote, "The Bible is full of Truth. You can spend your whole life studying it, and it still will be fresh and wonderful." (MacArthur, Faith, 74)

D.L. Moody stated there are four things necessary for studying the Bible: admit, submit, commit and transmit. First, admit its truth; second, submit to its teachings; third, commit it to memory; and fourth, transmit it." (Moody, Pleasures, 51) John W. Stott cautioned, "If we come to Scripture with our minds made up, expecting to hear from it only an echo of our own thoughts and never the thunderclap of God's, then indeed he will not speak to us and we shall only be confirmed in our own prejudices. We must allow the Word of God to confront us, to disturb our security, to undermine our complacency and to overthrow our patterns of thought and behavior." (Stott, <u>Culture and the Bible</u>, 33) J. I. Packer remarked, "If I were the devil, one of my first aims would be to stop folk from digging into the Bible. Knowing that it is the Word of God, teaching men to know and love and serve the God of the Word, I should do all I could to surround it with the spiritual equivalent of pits, thorn hedges, and man traps, to frighten people off...At all costs I should want to keep them from using their minds in a disciplined way to get the measure of the message." (Whitney 61) Satan certainly attempts to accomplish this objective in the believer's life and must be thwarted through a disciplined regiment of Bible Study that is steadfast and unshakeable.

John Stott wrote, "Some honor the Word and neglect the Spirit who alone can interpret it; others honor the Spirit but neglect the Word out of which he teaches. The only safeguard against lies is to have remaining within us both the Word that 'we heard from the beginning' and the anointing that we received from him. It is by these old possessions, not by new teachings or teachers that we shall remain in the truth." (Stott, <u>Letters of John</u>, 119)

At Yellowstone National Park dozens of small bears die each winter after tourist season waiting along the highway for a hand-out. No one comes to feed them and they die. Christians must not wait on others to instruct about Jesus or teach the scripture or else they will not grow spiritually. (2 Timothy 2:15)

Keys to Effective Bible Study
1. Study it through. Never start a day without "dissecting" a segment of Holy Scripture. (Psalm 39:3)
2. Pray it in. Digest what you dissect through prayer.
3. Put it down. Record in a journal the truth and lesson gained from the text studied. The palest ink is better than the best retentive memory.
4. Work it out. Flesh out the truth of the text studied throughout the day.
5. Pass it on. Endeavor to tell others what was learned in your Bible study.
(Adapted from Unknown Source)

METHODS OF BIBLE STUDY

As with the use of any study method, it is important to make personal application of the scriptural text. During Bible study ask, "What does this reveal about Jesus? What is the context of the text? What is the main lesson it teaches? In light of this text what action should I take?" Whatever God makes paramount in His Word He expects to be prominent in the life of the believer. Keep in mind that simply reading the Bible is not Bible Study. Bible Study involves dissection and application of a scriptural text. Max Lucado emphasized this truth: *"Search and you will find* is the pledge. The Bible is not a newspaper to be skimmed but rather a mine to be quarried. *Search for it like silver, and hunt for it like hidden treasure. Then you will understand respect for the* LORD, *and you will find that you know God* (Proverbs 2:4)." (Lucado, Life Lessons, 6) "Because Christ is the fixed point of reference for theology, we are concerned with how the text relates to Christ and how we relate to Christ." (Goldsworthy) It is essential that the believer lay aside personal prejudices, convictions, and notions in approaching scripture, allowing the Word to freely speak for itself without the hindrance of preconceived interpretation or understanding.

Reading a Scriptural Passage repetitively. Read a book of the Bible five times and then engage in its study. Repetitive reading prior to actual study will result in clearer illumination of the text's theme. In initiating the study of the Bible book, Dr. A. T. Pearson suggests searching out five P's: place where written, person by whom written, people to whom written, purpose for which written, period at which written. (Moody, Pleasures, 79) Next, capsulize into a few sentences the central meaning of each chapter and how it applies to the believer's life.

Study the Bible thematically. Study a theme such as "grace," "holiness," or "the second coming."

Study the Bible doctrinally. Study a doctrine of belief such as the "Deity of Christ," "Blood Atonement," "the Resurrection of Christ," or "Judgment."

Study the Miracles of the Bible. The list of miracles in the Bible exceeds 120, including the miraculous draught of fishes (Luke 5:4-11), the raising of the widow's son at Nain (Luke 7:11-18), the woman with the spirit of infirmity (Luke 13:11-17), the man with the dropsy (Luke 14:1-6), the ten lepers (Luke 17:11-19), and the healing of Malchus (Luke 22:50-51).

Study the Parables. Over one-third of Jesus' teaching in the Bible is comprised of parables. A parable is an earthly story or example that illustrates or teaches a spiritual truth. Jesus' parables include Matthew 7:24-28; 9:16-18; 11:16-17; 13:3-10; 13:24-31; 13:33; 13:44; Mark 4:26 -29; Luke 6:39-42 and John 15:1-7.

Study Biblical Prophecy. The study of prophecy undergirds and strengthens the believer in substantiating the authority of Holy Scripture. (2 Peter 1:19) How many people would it take flipping a quarter before one of them would hit heads thirty times in a row? (One billion) Did you know that of the thirty recorded prophecies concerning the birth, the death, and the resurrection of Jesus Christ all were fulfilled by Him? That's a lot of "heads in a row," isn't it? Prophecy affirms the deity of Jesus Christ. From 81 passages in the Old Testament, the New Testament lists 52 prophecies fulfilled in Jesus' birth and death. Each validate Jesus' claim as both Lord and Savior.

Study Great Bible Words. Engage in a study on biblical words like "justification," "repentance," "glorification," and "sanctification."

Study by Scripture Memory. "Thy word have I hid in mine heart, that I might not sin against thee." (Psalm 119:11) Scripture verses will keep you from spiritual reverses. John Trapp stated, "He hath a Bible in his head, and another in his heart; he hath a good treasure within, and there hence bringeth good things." (Spurgeon, The Treasury of David, 213) I have found it helpful to type out memory verses onto small stock size cards that can be put on a key ring. This method enables me to review verses previously learned while working on a new verse. The Navigators have an excellent scripture memory plan. (navigators.org)

Billy Graham's devotional method

"My wife and I read from the Psalms every day – five Psalms and one chapter of Proverbs. The Psalms teach you how to get along with God; Proverbs teaches you how to get along with people." (Graham, Life Wisdom, 102)

How to Read the Bible (C.H. Spurgeon)

"We are not always fit, it seems to me, to read the Bible. At times it were well for us to stop before we open the volume. "Put off thy shoe from thy foot, for the place whereon thou standest is holy ground." You have just come in from careful thought and anxiety about your worldly business, and you cannot immediately take that book and enter into its heavenly mysteries. As you ask a blessing over your meat before you fall to, so it would be a good rule for you to ask a blessing on the word before you partake of its heavenly food. Pray the Lord to strengthen your eyes before you dare to look into the eternal light of Scripture. As the priests washed their feet at the laver before they went to their holy work, so it were well to wash the soul's eyes with which you look upon God's word, to wash even the fingers, if I may so speak—the mental fingers with which you will turn from page to page—that with a holy book you may deal after a holy fashion. Say to your soul—"Come, soul, wake up: thou art not now about to read the newspaper; thou art not now perusing the pages of a human poet to be dazzled by his flashing poetry; thou art coming very near to God, who sits in the Word like a crowned monarch in his halls. Wake up, my glory; wake up, all that is within me. Though just now I may not be praising and glorifying God, I am about to consider that which should lead me so to do, and therefore it is an act of devotion. So be on the stir, my soul: be on the stir, and bow not sleepily before the awful throne of the Eternal." Scripture reading is our spiritual meal time. Sound the gong and call in every faculty to the Lord's own table to feast upon the precious meat which is now to be partaken of; or, rather, ring the church-bell as for worship, for the studying of the Holy Scripture ought to be as solemn a deed as when we lift the psalm upon the Sabbath day in the courts of the Lord's house." (Spurgeon, "How to Read")

TOOLS THAT ASSIST IN BIBLE STUDY

A Bible dictionary, concordance, commentary, journal for recording lessons learned, and a good study Bible are recommended *tools* for Bible study.

References and Commentaries
Cruden's Bible Dictionary
Halley's Handbook on the Bible
What the Bible is All About, Henrietta Mears
Nelson's Quick Reference (Chapter by Chapter Commentary),
    Warren Wiersbe
Young's Analytical Concordance
Vincent Word Studies of the New Testament
Matthew Henry's One Volume Commentary of the Bible
The Believer's Bible Commentary, William MacDonald
The Bible Knowledge Commentary, John F. Walvoord and
    Roy B. Zuck (Editors)
More Evidence that Demands a Verdict, Josh McDowell

Devotional Classics
Morning and Evening, C.H. Spurgeon
My Utmost for His Highest, Oswald Chambers
Streams in the Desert, L.B. Cowman

Bible Study Workbooks
Following God Series, Wayne Barber, Eddie Rasnake,
    Richard Shephard (AMG International)
Experiencing God, Henry Blackaby

Spiritual Classics
The Best of A.W. Tozer, Warren Wiersbe
Absolute Surrender, Andrew Murray
Abide in Christ, Andrew Murray
Spiritual Lessons, J. Oswald Sanders
The Practice of Godliness, Jerry Bridges
The Three-Fold Secret of the Holy Spirit, James McConkey
    (out of print)

DEFINITIONS OF BIBLE STUDY REFERENCES

Bible Atlases show geographical locations of Bible texts.

Bible Dictionaries define Bible words and serve as an encyclopedia on Bible subjects.

Bible Handbooks give an overview (survey) of Bible Books and chapters.

Commentaries provide interpretation and explanation of biblical texts, some with sermon outlines.

Concordances list all the words in the Bible, the texts in which they are found and original meaning.

Interlinear Bibles cite the Hebrew – Greek text between the lines of the English rendering.

Lexicons deal with Hebrew and Greek words defining their meaning.

Topical Bibles provides listing of Biblical texts that illumine the meaning of key words.

Word Studies provide background, original meaning and cultural usage of words.

THE PLACE FOR BIBLE STUDY

A definite place for Bible Study must be established. This place should be a *secluded place* free from interruptions and disturbances. This place should be a *special place* where there is "no horsing around." It is a place where the Christian meets the Creator of the world and his personal Savior. This place should be a *sacred place* of awe and holiness where the "brush of angel wings are felt all around." This place should be a *scheduled place* where the Christian meets God routinely at the same time. Hurry is the death of Bible Study. Schedule adequate time to read and muse over a scriptural text sifting from it all that it is ready to yield.

Three Stages of Bible Study
1. Caster Oil Stage. You do your Bible Study like taking bad tasting medicine because you know it is good for you not because you really want to.
2. Shredded Wheat Stage. You find Bible Study dry and bland but nourishing.
3. Peaches and Cream Stage. This is the stage where you really look forward to Bible Study. It is both a desire and delight. (Unknown source)

Digging Deeper

1. Why is the intake of God's Word on a regular basis imperative?
2. What is the lesson conveyed from the story of the little bears in Yellowstone National Park?
3. What are the eight methods of Bible Study listed in this chapter?
4. What are the 'tools' necessary for thorough Bible Study?
5. What is the significance of having a special place for Bible Study?

6

BAPTISM

"... My baptism reminds me whose I am and whom I must serve; who it is that stands pledged to love and cherish me, and share with me eternally all that he has; and what love and loyalty I owe in return." J. I. Packer (Packer 144)

The first thing a person is to do after becoming a Christian is to be baptized. (Matthew 28: 18-20; Acts 2:38) Baptism is one of the two ordinances or prescribed religious practices (the Lord's Supper being the other) that Jesus gave the church.

> "'Well,' says one, 'I do not think that I shall confess Christ; the dying thief did not confess him, did he? He was not baptized.' No, but he was a dying thief, recollect; and if you are not baptized, I think that you will be a living thief; for you will rob God of his glory, you will rob his servant also of the comfort which he ought to receive." C.H. Spurgeon (Spurgeon, "Dying Thief")

WHAT BAPTISM SAYS FOR THE SAINT

My wedding band says loudly three things. It declares I love somebody: Mary, my wife; I belong to somebody: Mary, my wife; and I submit to somebody: Mary, my wife. Baptism states the same three things. It says to friends, family and others, "I belong to and love somebody: Jesus Christ." In baptism the believer is shouting, "Now I belong to Jesus, and Jesus belongs to me. Not for the years of time alone but for all eternity." It declares, "I submit to somebody: Jesus Christ to do all He asks." Baptism tells people what happened at the moment of salvation. As believers go under and come up from the water, baptism pictures how Jesus washed their sins away and their new life in Christ. As the wedding ring is a symbol of my marital union with Mary, baptism is a symbol of one's union with Christ. I am not married simply because I wear this ring. A person may wear a ring and not be married. Just so, one is not saved or becomes a Christian by being baptized or confirmed or christened. It is possible to be baptized and not be a child of God just like Simon Magus. (Acts 8:13-23) Scripture is clear that before a person is baptized he must first be saved or else what he is saying in being baptized is not true.

WHAT BAPTISM SAYS ABOUT THE SAVIOR

Baptism is a picture of what happened to Jesus on Good Friday through Easter morning. Lowering a person into the water tells how Jesus died on the Cross for man's sin and was buried. Holding the person under the water tells how Jesus was in the grave for three days. Raising the person out of the water tells of Jesus' victorious resurrection. This symbolism can only be depicted through the New Testament mode of baptism by immersion. Baptism tells of what Jesus did before, on, and after the Cross. He willingly allowed soldiers to place a crown of jagged thorns upon His head, hammer nails into His feet and hands, pluck hair from His face, compel Him to carry a Cross to Calvary, and then pierce His side with a sword. Jesus suffered much because of His love for the world. Upon the Cross, Jesus prayed, "Father forgive them for they know not what they do," (Luke 23:34) referencing all those responsible for His crucifixion and manifesting nothing but love even for His enemies. The body of Jesus was buried and sealed in the tomb of Joseph and guarded by Roman soldiers. (Matthew 27:65) On the third day (Easter morning), the stone was rolled away by God and Jesus was raised from the dead. (Luke 24:6) Jesus revealed Himself unto many people for the next forty days before going back to Heaven. The resurrection appearances of Christ include Mary Magdalene (John 20: 11-18); other women (Matthew 28:9, 10); two disciples on Emmaus Road (Luke 24: 13-35); ten disciples (John 20: 19-25); Thomas (John 20: 26-31); seven disciples on the Sea of Galilee (John 21: 1 – 25); at the Great Commission (Matthew 28: 16-20); feeding the five hundred (I Corinthians 15:6); His ascension (Acts 1: 9-10); Paul (Acts 9: 3-6); and to John (Revelation 1:10-18). Baptism says for Jesus, "I *am* he that liveth, and was dead; and, behold, I am alive for evermore, Amen; and have the keys of hell and of death." (Revelation 1:18) The church awaits His return.

WHAT BAPTISM SAYS TO THE SINNER
Baptism not only speaks for the saint and about the Savior, but it also speaks to the sinner. Baptism says clearly that Jesus loves the unsaved so very much that He paid the ultimate price of death upon a Cross for their salvation. "For this *is* good and acceptable in the sight of God our Savior; who will have all men to be saved, and to come unto the knowledge of the truth. For there is one God, and one mediator between God and men, the man Christ Jesus; who gave himself a ransom for all, to be testified in due time." (I Timothy 2: 3-6) Sin separated man from God, but Jesus

through Calvary became man's mediator or bridge to God. Through the Cross man can be reconciled (made right) with God. Baptism tells the message of God's awesome love and sacrifice for the world. "For God so loved the world that He gave His only begotten son that whosoever believeth on Him should not perish but have everlasting life." (John 3:16)

WHAT SCRIPTURE SAYS ABOUT BAPTISM

The Bible says only those who are saved may be baptized. (Acts 2:38) The Bible says that immediately following a person's conversion he should be baptized. (Acts 8: 35-39) The Bible says failure for a believer to be baptized is an act of disobedience. Un-baptized believers are unable to live with a "clear conscience" before God. (I Peter 3:21) The Bible says age is not a factor in relation to baptism, but salvation is. A believer need only be baptized once and that is immediately after being *Born Again*. (Acts 16:31-33) The Bible declares baptism is not proof of salvation. (Acts 8: 13, 23) The Bible states that baptism is not essential to salvation. (Romans 10:13; Ephesians 2:8-9) Warren Wiersbe commented, "If baptism is essential for salvation, then nobody in the Old Testament was ever saved, for there was no baptism under the Law. Christ came to save, yet He did not baptize (John 4:2). If baptism is necessary for eternal life, why did Paul rejoice because he had not baptized more people? (1 Corinthians 1:13–17)." (Wiersbe, Expository Commentary on the New Testament, John 3: 6-7) There is no need to fear baptism. A pastor should take every measure possible to make baptism worshipful and worry free.

HOW TO BE BAPTIZED

At the conclusion of a church worship service an invitation to respond to the message preached will be extended. It is at this point that a person may approach the pastor indicating a desire to follow the Lord in obedience to baptism. He will arrange a time for the baptism.

Digging Deeper
1. What is the analogy used between the wedding ring and baptism?
2. Does Baptism have power to cleanse of sin and to save?
3. What does Baptism picture?
4. Who ought to be baptized?
5. Why should a person be baptized?

7

THE LORD'S SUPPER

"In order that we might remember Him, Jesus didn't ask for a monument to be erected or a holiday to be established. He asked that a meal be enjoyed." Jon Courson (<u>Courson,</u> I Corinthians 11: 23-26)

In essence, the two elements of the Lord's Supper given in Luke 22-18-19 ("bread," representing Jesus' broken body and "the fruit of the vine," representing Jesus' spilt blood), point to the physical incarnation, sacrificial death, triumphant resurrection, and second coming of Jesus Christ. Neither element in any way transmits grace or cleansing of sin to the recipient. The Bible cites no frequency for the observance of this Supper but simply states, "For as often as ye eat this bread, and drink this cup, ye do show the Lord's death till he come." (Luke 22:26) The believer is only worthy to partake of this Supper based not upon personal merit but his relationship with Jesus Christ. Jesus welcomes all His children to *His* table (not the table of a church or a denomination).

PICTURES OF THE LORD'S SUPPER
(I CORINTHIANS 11: 17 – 34)

The Lord's Supper pictures Christ. "This do in remembrance of me." The Lord's Supper is all about the sacrificial death of Jesus on Calvary, and that is what is to be pondered and reflected upon deeply when the Lord's Supper is taken. It is with great significance that Jesus tells believers to remember that it was He, the sinless Son of God, who paid the ultimate price for man's salvation. Apart from Him salvation is not possible. Jesus is saying, "As oft as you come to my table do not forget what I did at Calvary out of love for you."

It pictures Calvary. The Lord's Supper not only reveals the fact of Jesus' death but the manner of His death. He willingly laid down His life at Calvary, bearing its excruciating pain and death because of His love for the world. This ordinance speaks of the crown of thorns upon His brow; the nails that pierced His hands and feet; the sword that was thrust into His side; the spit that was hurled upon Him, and all the accusations railed against Him. All of these He endured to secure our salvation. We know this was His agony, but what about the "Unknown suffering" Jesus bore in the inner chamber of the heart! And He says to you and me, "Remember this. Don't ever forget that!" The "bread and the fruit of the vine" clearly declare, "Remember Calvary and all Jesus bore there for man's forgiveness of sin." I remember donating blood to a teenager named Paul years ago. He was in desperate need of my type of blood. Afterward he said, "Frank, thank you for the blood." My blood enabled his life. As we look at Calvary let's remember His shed blood that was poured out to enable us to have life abundant and eternal. Let us come to the table saying, "Jesus, thank you for the blood."

It pictures Celebration. The Lord's Supper is a feast, not a funeral! It's a celebration party concerning all Christ did for mankind at Calvary. Everything it says speaks of joy and hope. Matthew's account of the Lord's Supper states that this celebration included singing. (Matthew 26:30) Let the redeemed of the Lord *sing* about His table songs of praise and adoration like E.M. Bartlett's "Victory in Jesus."

I heard an old, old story how a Savior came from glory
How He gave His life on Calvary, to save a wretch like me.
I heard about His groaning, and His precious blood atoning
Then I repented of my sin and won the victory.

In coming to this table celebrate Jesus and what He has done that none other could do for you.

It pictures Communion. Five times in this biblical text the apostle refers to the "coming together" of believers. (1 Corinthians 11: 17, 18, 20, 33, 34) The Lord's Supper is a time when God's people are truly united in focus and fellowship as they sit at *one* table; partake of *one* meal, and drink of *one* cup. The Lord's Supper pictures Christ's desire for the church to be *one* in devotion, doctrine, and duty exhibiting love *one* to another.

It pictures Commission. No clearer gospel message could be presented than Jesus' use of the bread and cup in speaking of man's salvation. It is a visible sermon of the message and meaning of the Cross. It is a testimony to those who do not love Jesus of God's awesome love for them. The Lord's Supper teaches and reminds believers to proclaim its message to the world.

It pictures Consummation. Jesus will come back to take those who love Him to His home in Heaven ("Till I come."). This is a promise Jesus will keep. (I John 3: 2-3) When coming to this table, believers are exhorted to "Look up for your redemption draweth nigh." (Luke 21:28)

It pictures Confession. Preparation that includes self-examination is required as the believer prepares to partake of this meal for it is to be observed with clean hands, pure heart, and proper motive. (1 Corinthians 11:27-29) This examination often reveals acts of sin that must be confessed to Christ and cleansed before taking the elements. (1 John 1:9) Jesus welcomes to the table all His children who meet this condition. In observing the Lord's Supper, remember these seven things with gratitude to Jesus for all He did to make possible "salvation so rich and free."

"*Unworthy manner* (11:27): ritualistically, indifferently, with an unrepentant heart, a spirit of bitterness, or any other ungodly attitude." John MacArthur (MacArthur, Study Bible, 1 Corinthians 11:27)

Guard against this Supper becoming mundane, ritualistic, and mere formality. On a dirt road deep in the country a boy riding his bicycle was struck by a car and was killed. An older brother said, "Later, when my father picked up the mangled twisted bike, I heard him sob out loud for the first time in my life. He carried it to the barn and placed it in a spot we seldom used. Father's terrible sorrow eased with the passing of time, but for many years whenever he saw that bike, tears began streaming down his face." The older brother continued, "Since then I have often prayed, 'Lord, keep the memory of Your death as fresh as that to me! Every time I partake of Your memorial supper, let my heart be stirred as though You died only yesterday. Never let the communion services become a mere formality, but always a tender and touching experience.'" This prayer of the older brother ought to be that of every believer with regard to the Lord's Supper.

Digging Deeper
1. What is the seven-fold picture of the Lord's Supper?
2. What do the two elements of this ordinance represent?
3. Does the Lord's Supper possess saving power? Why or why not?
4. Who may participate in the Lord's Supper?

8

STEWARDSHIP

"One of the greatest missing teachings in the American church today is the reminder to men and women that nothing we have belongs to us." Gordon MacDonald (MacDonald)

"When it comes to giving until it hurts, most people have a very low threshold of pain." (Anonymous)

"If a person gets his attitude toward money straight, it will help straighten out almost every other area in his life." Billy Graham (Myra 107)

"Money never stays with me. It would burn me if it did. I throw it out of my hands as soon as possible, lest it should find its way into my heart." John Wesley (Tompkins 167)

A steward is one entrusted to manage possessions that are not his own. Every Christian is a steward of God regarding his body, health, money, ability, gifts, and time and as such is entrusted with their wisest and most biblical use. (Psalm 24:1) The Apostle Paul declared, "Moreover it is required in stewards, that a man be found faithful." (1 Corinthians 4:2) Solomon instructed, "Be not wise in thine own eyes: fear the LORD, and depart from evil. It shall be health to thy navel, and marrow to thy bones. Honour the LORD with thy substance, and with the firstfruits of all thine increase: So shall thy barns be filled with plenty, and thy presses shall burst out with new wine." *(*Proverbs 3:7-10)

The Macedonian Christians serve as a pattern of New Testament stewardship. (2 Corinthians 8: 1-15)

THEY GAVE THEMSELVES

"But first they gave their own selves to the Lord". (v 5) The priority of these early saints was to make a total presentation of body, mind and soul unto God. (Romans 12: 1-2) Herein lays the foundation of biblical stewardship on which the *grace* of giving springs. As the offering was being taken during a revival in Africa, a brand-new Christian told the deacon holding the collection plate to put it lower. "Lower, lower, lower," he said—until the offering plate was on the ground. Then he stood up and stepped in. This man understood. This brand-new believer got the picture. He gave himself. (Courson, 2 Corinthians 8:5) All believers are to follow this example. Through personal dedication to God there will come a disciplined use of a believer's treasure, time, talent, and the total essence of all he possesses for Kingdom purposes.

THEY GAVE EAGERLY

"They begged us again and again for the privilege of sharing in the gift for the believers in Jerusalem." (v 4, NLT) The Macedonian saints literally begged for the privilege to financially help the believers in Jerusalem and viewed doing so as an honor not an obligation. As a young student pastor, I encountered this attitude in a widow of our church who would beg me to take her monetary gifts from time to time.

She longed to help her pastor financially and would not take "no" for an answer. This attitude of eagerly wanting to give to the cause of Christ through a missionary, evangelist, ministerial student, the poor, and local church is one all believers must exhibit, taking advantage of every opportunity to help God's work financially. You may not always be able to fully meet a financial or material need in the church or a ministry but steadfastly maintain an attitude of eagerness to do what is possible. A young man received a bright red shiny car as a gift. A poor little boy asked him, "Mister, where did you get that bright red shiny car?" The youth responded, "My brother gave it to me." Thinking the little boy would say, "Boy, I wish I had a brother like that" he was shocked to hear the reply, "Boy, I wish I could be a brother like that." This little boy expressed the right attitude regarding giving.

THEY GAVE SACRIFICIALLY

"They are being tested by many troubles, and they are very poor. But they are also filled with abundant joy, which has overflowed in rich generosity." (v 2, NLT) Though experiencing great troubles and deep poverty, the Macedonian saints sacrificed greatly in order to meet the need in Jerusalem. Financial giving will always be a sacrifice because it involves the denial of personal, family, or business gain to some extent. Giving should always cost the giver something. King David, following a plague in Israel, was instructed to build an altar upon the threshing floor of Araunah and offer upon it sacrifices to God. Araunah offered to give the property and oxen for the sacrifice to David without charge. David responded unto Araunah, "Nay; but I will surely buy *it* of thee at a price: neither will I offer burnt offerings unto the LORD my God of that which doth cost me nothing. So David bought the threshing floor and the oxen for fifty shekels of silver. And David built there an altar unto the LORD, and offered burnt offerings and peace offerings." (2 Samuel 24: 24 -25) King

David refused to give unto God that which cost him nothing. In giving measure the gift's size and worthiness by what it cost to give. C.H. Spurgeon remarked, "Our gifts are not to be measured by the amount we contribute, but by the surplus kept in our own hands. The two mites of the widow were, in Christ's eyes, worth more than all the other money cast into the treasury, for "she of her want did cast in all she had, even all her living." (C.H. Spurgeon, "The Best Donation")

Ultimately, the sacrifice Christ made for man's salvation is the believer's impetus and inspiration for sacrificial giving. How generous was Christ? Paul answers, "For ye know the grace of our Lord Jesus Christ, that, though he was rich, yet for your sakes he became poor, that ye through his poverty might be rich." (2 Corinthians 8:9) He was the most generous person who ever lived. "He was rich in possessions, power, homage, fellowship, happiness. He became poor in station, circumstances, in His relations with men. We are urged to give a little money, clothing, and food. He gave Himself." (MacDonald and Farstad, 2 Corinthians 8:9) John MacArthur remarked, "He laid aside the independent exercise of all His divine prerogatives, left His place with God, took on human form, and died on a Cross like a common criminal, *that you. . . might become rich.* Believers become spiritually rich through the sacrifice and impoverishment of Christ. They become rich in salvation, forgiveness, joy, peace, glory, honor, and majesty. They become joint heirs with Christ." (MacArthur, 2 Corinthians 8:9)

Isaac Watts expressed Christ's sacrifice and man's only reasonable response in the hymn "When I Survey the Wondrous Cross."

When I survey the wondrous Cross
On which the Prince of glory died,
My richest gain I count but loss,
And pour contempt on all my pride.

See from His head, His hands, His feet,
Sorrow and love flow mingled down!
Did e'er such love and sorrow meet,
Or thorns compose so rich a crown?

Were the whole realm of nature mine,
That were a present far too small;
Love so amazing, so divine,
Demands my soul, my life, my all.

THEY GAVE EXPECTANTLY
"Fellowship of the ministering of the saints." (v 4)The
Macedonia saints believed God would use their gift to help
the suffering believers of Jerusalem and at the same time
supply their needs personally. (Philippians 4:19) Faithful
giving not only advances the gospel but benefits the giver.
"Give, and it shall be given unto you; good measure, pressed
down, and shaken together, and running over, shall men give
into your bosom. For with the same measure that ye mete
withal it shall be measured to you again." (Luke 6:38) John
Bunyan in <u>Pilgrims Progress</u> stated, "A man there was and
they called him mad; for the more he gave the more he had."
Solomon declares, "The liberal soul shall be made fat: and
he that watereth shall be watered also himself." (Proverbs
11:25) The Macedonian saints were "fat." A person cannot
out give God. Captain Levy was asked how he could give so
much to the Lord's work and still possess great wealth. The
Captain replied, "Oh, as I shovel it out, He shovels it in, and
the Lord has a bigger shovel." (<u>Today in the Word</u> 28) C.H.
Spurgeon testified, "In all of my years of service to my Lord,
I have discovered a truth that has never failed and has never
been compromised. That truth is that it is beyond the realm
of possibilities that one has the ability to out give God. Even
if I give the whole of my worth to Him, He will find a way

to give back to me much more than I gave." (churchonline. com)

THEY GAVE JOYOUSLY

"The abundance of their joy." (v 2) The Macedonian saints did not give out of legal obligation or grudgingly but joyously. The privilege of financially supporting the cause of Christ locally and globally should bring joy to the heart of the believer. Paul admonishes, "Every man according as he purposeth in his heart, *so let him give*; not grudgingly, or of necessity: for God loveth a cheerful giver." (2 Corinthians 9:7) "You must each decide in your heart how much to give. Don't give reluctantly or in response to pressure. For God loves a person who gives cheerfully." (2 Corinthians 9:7, NLT)

THEY GAVE WILLINGLY

"They were willing of themselves." (v 3) These saints were not pressed to give but gave willingly. A farmer was asked, "How much milk does your cow give?" He replied, "If you mean voluntarily contribution, then she doesn't give anything, but we take from her eleven quarts a day." A cartoon shows Charles being baptized and the pastor saying to him, "Everything that goes under the water belongs to God." As the pastor lowers Charles under the water one can see his hand extending out of the water clutching a wallet. Charles was not willing to give of his treasure to the Lord. A lecturer in using his strength and awesome grip completed his lectures by squeezing an orange of all its juice. He then would challenge his audience, "I will give $25 to anyone who can squeeze this orange and get any more juice out of it." Many tried in various cities but failed until a man who did not appear very strong succeeded. Shocked, the lecturer asked the man "You don't look that strong. How in the world were you able to do that? What kind of work do you do?"

The man responded, "I am a Baptist preacher. I have a lot of practice squeezing things!" Saints ought to give willingly not out of human compulsion or induced guilt.

THEY GAVE LOVINGLY

"I am not commanding you but testing the genuineness of your love by the enthusiasm of others." (v 8, ISV) The giving of the Macedonian Christians evidenced their love for God, and so it will be the test of all believers regarding the sincerity of their love for Him. The measure of biblical giving is determined by the believer's love for God. C.H. Spurgeon remarked, "Giving is true loving." (Council on Foundations) Price Kellam, a saintly deacon in my seminary student pastorate, refused to claim his financial gifts to the Lord's work as a tax deduction despite my effort to have him do otherwise. To him claiming tax deductibility would have contaminated his motive of giving which was solely based upon love for God. It has been said and I believe it to be true, "Real charity doesn't care if it's tax deductible or not." In giving, stay focused upon the recipient, Jesus Christ. You are giving to the King of Kings; churches and ministries are merely conduits authorized by Him to receive and disburse His money.

THEY GAVE SYSTEMATICALLY

Paul did not specifically address the manner in which the Macedonian Christians were to give in I Corinthians 8, but it goes to reason they were to give and did give as he instructed the Galatians and others regarding the same offering for the suffering Christians in Jerusalem who were hit hard by a famine. In 1 Corinthians 16: 1-2 Paul states regarding this offering, "Now concerning the collection for the saints, as I have given order to the churches of Galatia, even so do ye. Upon the first *day* of the week let every one of you lay by him in store, as *God* hath prospered him, that there be no gatherings when I come." Note Paul's three-fold instruction regarding their giving. It was to be received systematically on the *first day of the week*, Sunday. It was to be corporate giving; *everyone* was to participate in the offering. It was to be proportionate giving; the amount was to be based on how God *hath prospered him*, in keeping with his income and resources. This provides guidance to all believers regarding *giving* to the Lord; giving should be intentional and systematic, and all are to give and giving should be based upon the measure in which God has financially blessed. Many churches provide members with offering envelopes to assist in regular, consistent giving.

George Muller remarked, "Are you giving *systematically* to the Lord's work, or are you leaving it to feeling, to impression made upon you through particular circumstances, or to striking appeals? If we do not give from principle *systematically*, we shall find that our one brief life is gone before we are aware of it, and that, in return, we have done little for that adorable One who bought us with His precious blood, and to whom belongs all we have and are." (Whitney 150)

THE STARTING BLOCK FOR GIVING IS THE TITHE

In the Old Testament there were several mandatory tithes the people were to give to the Lord; the Levite's (10 percent, Malachi 3:10), the Festival (10 percent, Deuteronomy 12:10-11) and the Poor (3 percent, Deuteronomy 14:28-29). Additionally the people were to give free will offerings for special projects. These combined reveal that the people of God in the Old Testament were giving between 27 to 40 percent of their income to His work. (Hughes) A good starting place for the believer in giving is thirty percent less than what these contributed, the tithe (ten percent) of income. Billy Graham stated, "The Bible teaches tithing. A tithe is one tenth of your income. That one-tenth of your income belongs to the Lord. In addition to your tithe, you should give as the Lord has prospered you." (Graham 40) Galatians 3:24 says "The law is a tutor to lead us toward Christ." The tithe as part of the Old Testament Law serves as a teacher prompting the believer to start with ten percent of income ever seeking to give more. The tithe is the *floor* level of giving not the *ceiling*. (Haggai 2:8) "Much has been said of giving a tenth of one's income to the Lord. I think that is a Christian duty which none should, for a moment, question. If it was a duty under the Jewish Law, much more is it so now under the Christian dispensation." (Spurgeon, "A Cheerful Giver") "So the question is not, 'How much of my money should I give to God?' but rather, 'How much of God's money should I keep for myself?' When we put a check or cash in the offering plate, we should give it with the belief that *all* we have belongs to God and with a commitment that we will use *all* of it as He wants." (Whitney 139) Christians need to learn to live with less so that more money may be given to evangelism and mission endeavors.

> "I do not believe one can settle how much we ought to give. I am afraid the only safe rule is to give more than we can spare." C.S. Lewis (Complete Lewis 52)

THE VALUE OF GIVING

The profit of giving is clearly presented in scripture.

Giving pleases the Savior. The widow in giving two mites pleased the Lord. (Mark 12:42-43) The woman of Bethany in anointing Jesus' feet with a box of ointment pleased the Lord. (Luke 7:37-47) The little boy in giving his loaves and fishes pleased the Lord. (John 6:9-13) In these cases the individuals gave what they could give. Christ is pleased when His children give what they can "according to how God hath prospered him." (1 Corinthians 16:2)

Giving provides the saint. The giver has a clear scriptural promise that biblical giving result in bountiful provision. Jesus declares, "Give, and it shall be given unto you; good measure, pressed down, and shaken together, and running over, shall men give into your bosom. For with the same measure that ye mete withal it shall be measured to you again." (Luke 6:38) Matthew Henry commented, "*Men* shall *return it into your bosom* (lap); for God often makes use of *men* as instruments, not only of his *avenging,* but of his *rewarding* justice. If we in a right manner give to others when they need, God will incline the hearts of others to give to us when we need, and to give liberally, *good measure pressed down and shaken together.* They that *sow plentifully* shall *reap plentifully.*" (Henry, Commentary on the Whole Bible) In Malachi 3:8-10 God promises to open the windows of heaven upon the giver pouring out blessings to the extent "that there shall not be room enough to receive it." Solomon states, "There is that scattereth, and yet increaseth; and *there is* that withholdeth more than is meet, but *it tendeth* to poverty. The liberal soul shall be made fat: and he that watereth shall be watered also himself." (Proverbs 11:24-25) In essence these promises are stating the more you give, the more you will get. Note that in these texts cited God does not indicate the type of provision that will be exacted. The writer of Hebrews assures the giving saint, "God is fair; he will not forget the work you did and the love you showed for him by helping his people. And he will remember that you are still helping them." (Hebrews 6:10, NCV)

Giving produces souls. Liberal giving funds churches, missionaries, and evangelists, enabling the proclamation of the gospel locally and globally. A song by Ray Boltz speaks of the value of such giving in stating,

Then another man stood before you, he said "Remember
 the time,
A missionary came to your church, His pictures made
 you cry.
You didn't have much money but you gave it anyway.
Jesus took that gift you gave
And that's why I'm in Heaven today."

Give generously and regularly, because in so doing more souls will hear the Good News of Christ at home and abroad resulting in lives being eternally changed.

A story is told about a $100 bill and $1 bill on the way to the furnace (the place all old money is destined). The $1 bill asked the $100 bill how its life had been. "Really great," it replied, "I made a lot of trips to San Francisco, to the finest department stores and restaurants. Been good." It then asked the $1 bill, "How about your life?" The $1 bill replied, "My life was pretty much giving to church, giving to church, giving to church." Far too many saints generously give at restaurants, department stores and vacation resorts but so greedily to God's work.

In Luke 19:11-27 Jesus shares the parable of the talents. Upon a master's departure he entrusted one talent to the first servant, two talents to the second servant, and five talents to the third servant. Upon his return each of these servants had to give an account of how they used the money. It is a picture of Jesus Christ entrusting His children (servants) with money to handle Kingdom business. (Deuteronomy 8:18; James 1:17) He has departed for Heaven but upon His return an accounting will be made by every servant regarding the worthy or unworthy use of their (His) money. (Luke 19:13)

Digging Deeper
   1. Who is a steward?
   2. What is the foundational step to stewardship?

3. Name the three things stewardship encompasses in the believer's life?
4. In what ways are the Macedonian Christians a pattern for stewardship?
5. How much should a believer give to the cause of Christ?
6. What is the benefit of giving systematically?
7. What is the value of giving unto the Lord?
8. What is the message of the parable of the talents?

9

SATAN

"I often laugh at Satan, and there is nothing that makes him so angry as when I attack him to his face, and tell him that through God I am more than a match for him." Martin Luther (Luther <thinkexist>)

"The only time to stop temptation is at the first point of recognition. If one begins to argue and engage in a hand-to-hand combat, temptation almost always wins the day." Thomas a' Kempis (a' Kempis)

"And Satan himself uses a master stroke in his own behalf when he gets people to deny that he is – no matter what the Bible and Christ and the experience of all centuries of human history say." R.G. Lee (Lee)

Satan is for real. W.A. Criswell remarked, "He is called by his name 174 times in the Word of God. He's called Satan. He's called the Devil. He's called that old serpent. He's called the dragon. He's called Beelzebub. But in one or the other of those names, he's named in the Bible 100 times and he is presented as a person, a personality, as somebody, like God is somebody, like Michael is somebody, like Gabriel is somebody. This enemy of ours is somebody. Eve met him in Garden of Eden. Job had to do with him. He fell into the hands of Satan. Christ—and that's the reason we read our Scripture from the fourth of Matthew this morning—Christ had to do with him, a personal adversary. His name—Christ himself addressed him as Satan: 'Satan, get behind me!' A personal enemy." (Criswell, "Satan")

Upon salvation and renunciation of the old life of sin and religious formality, Satan cunningly seeks the believer's downfall vehemently. It is Satan's purpose to pull the new believer back down into the mire of sin from which he was rescued. Do not underestimate this enemy's power to bring a Christian down because if he could destroy a Samson, a David, and a Demas all are vulnerable. (Judges 16:18-21; 2 Samuel 11:3-5; 2 Timothy 4:10) Paul cautions "Let him that thinketh he standeth take heed lest he fall." (I Corinthians 10:12) Peter warns, "Be sober, be vigilant; because your adversary the devil, as a roaring lion, walketh about, seeking whom he may devour." (I Peter 5:8) The term "devil" means to "slander." Satan as the "slanderer" seeks to accuse Christians falsely before God and use the unsaved to do the same. Satan as a "serpent" seeks to deceive believers as he did Eve in the garden. (2 Corinthians 11:3) Satan as a 'lion' seeks to "devour" (totally consume) the believer's spiritual vitality, testimony, and witness. (1 Peter 5:8) Satan as the "well spring of lies" seeks to deceive man by counterfeiting salvation and "sugar coating" the consequence of a life apart from God. (John 8:44) Satan as the "destroyer" (Revelation 12:11) "seeks to kill, steal and destroy" the best of one's life. (John 10:10) Satan is relentless to shipwreck the believer's life and witness. Peter exhorts the believer to "resist Satan steadfastly in the faith." (I Peter 5:9) Christians must stay alert, watchful for Satan's ploys to trip him up by standing firm in the Word of God.

The schemes of the devil include lying (John 8:44); tempting (Matthew 4:1); robbing (Matthew 13:19); harassing (2 Corinthians 12:7); hindering (I Thessalonians 2:18); sifting (Luke 22:31); imitating (2 Corinthians 11: 14-15); accusing (Revelation 12: 9-10); smiting with disease (Luke 13:16); possessing (John 13:37); killing and devouring (John 8:44). Thomas Brooks warned, "Satan hath snares for the wise and snares for the simple; snares for the hypocrites and snares for the upright; snares for generous souls, and snares for timorous souls; snares for the rich and snares for the poor; snares for the aged and snares for youth. Happy are those souls that are not taken and held in the snares that he hath laid!" (Brooks 12)

VICTORY OVER SATAN

How can the Christian overcome the tactics of Satan? Ephesians 6:11-18 teaches that the believer can be victorious over Satan by putting on gospel armor daily. Football players wear a type of armor for protection on the gridiron and catchers wear it in the game of baseball. As a baseball catcher, I wore armor that consisted of a breast protector, shin guards, mask, and of course a glove. This armor kept me from serious injury and in the game. As athletes need armor for protection in the game they play, Ephesians 6 states that believers need spiritual armor for protection in the game of life.

The Belt of Truth speaks of the believer's need to live his belief. It is important the child of God daily study the Bible and seek to live out its teaching. This Belt held other pieces of the armor together for easy access by the soldier granting him freedom of movement. The Belt of Truth will hold the believer's life together when things shatter and crumble and Satan opposes granting freedom to press onward.

The Breastplate of Righteousness speaks of the need to start each day clean and holy. The believer's first act of business each morning is to get himself right before God. He is not to carry any soiled laundry (sin) into a new day but to start it fresh and pure.

The Gospel Shoes speak of the believer's assurance of salvation and disposition to recognize immediately one's duty with readiness to plunge into it. It is important the Christian soldier walk in full confidence of salvation so that in the time of doubt or temptation he will not stumble and fall. Confidence of salvation enables a life of peace in every circumstance of life, whether good or bad. Gospel shoes also remind saints of the need to share the Good News of the Gospel with the unsaved.

The Shield of Faith speaks of the need to always believe God. Genesis 3 records how Satan lied to Eve. "You won't die!" the serpent hissed. God knows that your eyes will be opened when you eat it. You will become just like God, knowing everything, both good and evil. The woman was convinced. The fruit looked so fresh and delicious, and it would make her so wise! So she ate some of the fruit." (Genesis 3:4-6, NLT) Eve believed Satan over God, the Shield came down, and sin entered the world. Don't be like Eve. Always believe God. Roman soldiers were responsible for providing some measure of protection for comrades in battle and thus they carried their shield with their left arm so it protected two-thirds of their body and one-third of the body of the solider on his left. Christians likewise are to render protection to each other by exhibiting conquering and encouraging faith.

The Helmet of Salvation speaks of the need to look at the finish line in Heaven. The Helmet of Salvation reminds believers there is a finish line ahead where Jesus waits for the saved. This part of the armor assures the believer of salvation and that one day he will be in the eternal presence of the King of Kings. This Helmet also protects one's mind from being dominated by carnal and sensual thoughts.

The Sword of the Spirit speaks of the power of the Holy Scripture needed in the believer's life. In the wilderness temptations, Jesus used the Sword of the Spirit (the Word of God) to drive back Satan, declaring, "It is written..." (Matthew 4:1-11) "It is written" is like a dagger to Satan's heart. During temptation, believers should quote Satan scripture that forces him to flee. This teaches the importance of scripture memorization. (Psalm 119: 11) John MacArthur stated, "There are no bounds for the Word of God because it is a divinely powerful, spiritually effective weapon. In Ephesians 6:17 Paul called it "the sword of the Spirit." The Greek word he used refers to a dagger anywhere from six to eighteen inches long. It was used...in hand-to-hand combat. The sword of the Spirit, therefore, is not a broadsword that you just flail around, hoping to do some damage. It is incisive; it must hit a vulnerable spot or it won't be effective." (MacArthur, How to Meet the Enemy, 141)

The Knees of Prayer speak of the utter futility of success in battle apart from divinely infused strength. The preacher George Allen Smith was standing on the precipice of a mountain in the Alps viewing Switzerland when a gushing wind suddenly arose that threatened to blow him over the edge. Immediately his guide cried out, "Mr. Smith! On your knees, sir! The only way you're safe up here is on your knees!" (Courson, Matthew 6:13) When battling Satan, the only way you're safe down here is on your knees. Paul instructs, "Praying always with all prayer and supplication in the Spirit, and watching thereunto with all perseverance." (Ephesians 6:18)

PRAYING ON THE ARMOR OF GOD
Pray on the pieces of the armor daily without allowing it to become merely a religious routine. I pray something like this:

"Heavenly Father thank you for the armor provided for my victory today. By faith I put on the Belt of Truth that I might live what I believe and advocate.

Keep me from being a castaway by helping to maintain my integrity. By faith I put on the Breastplate of Righteousness that I may start this day clean and holy prepared to live a life pleasing to you. By faith I put on the Gospel Shoes that I may be surefooted in battle against Satan assured of my salvation, eternal destiny and ever ready to serve. By faith I put on the Shield of Faith trusting you to extinguish the fiery darts of opposition that Satan hurls upon me. I will not fear what may happen today for thou art a shield of protection unto me. By faith I place the Helmet of Salvation upon my head to protect my mind from carnal thoughts and to focus upon the completion of my salvation in Heaven. Lord today I look for your coming and my departure to Heaven. By faith I pick up the Sword of the Spirit, thy Holy Word, to drive Satan back and to overcome temptation. By faith I pray each piece of this protective armor upon my life that I may be a victorious Christian soldier. Grant it O Lord I pray. Amen."

"If you are to be a soldier in this army, if you are to fight victoriously in this crusade, you have to put on the entire equipment given to you. That is a rule in any army. . . . And that is infinitely more true in this spiritual realm and warfare with which we are concerned . . . because your understanding is inadequate. It is God alone who knows your enemy, and He knows exactly the provision that is essential to you if you are to continue standing. Every single part and portion of this armour is absolutely essential; and the first thing you have to learn is that you are not in a position to pick and choose." Martyn Lloyd-Jones (Lloyd-Jones 179)

How often should the Christian put on this gospel armor? Daily. How? Prayerfully. What pieces of the armor are to be put on daily? All of it. Charles H. Spurgeon warned, "Your hearts may glow with a seraphic flame of love to Jesus, and yet the devil will try to bring you down to Laodicean lukewarmness. If you will tell me when God permits a Christian to lay aside his armor, I will tell you when Satan has left off temptation. Like the old knights in war time, we must sleep with helmet and breastplate buckled on, for the archdeceiver will seize our first unguarded hour to make us his prey. The Lord keep us watchful in all seasons, and give us a final escape from the jaw of the lion and the paw of the bear." (Spurgeon, <u>Morning</u>, Feb. 20)

The Gospel Armor
(Frank Shivers)

Christian warrior put on the Gospel Armor from head to toe
that victory may be won against Satan the able foe.

Belief and practice must agree, lest the believer be a poor witness of one set free.
This Belt of Truth prompts self-discipline in the spiritual fight
and enables the believer's *Light* to ever glow bright.

Purity in heart assure at days start, making it the goal not to depart.
This breastplate protection from despair due to sin will bring,
Prompting joyfulness, and fruitfulness unto the King.

Gospel shoes give security when peace about salvation is attacked,
Granting calm assurance it's a certain fact.

Faith is the victory that overcomes the world,
Raise this shield of defense when Satan's fiery arrows of doubt, difficulty and discouragement are hurled.

The helmet of salvation place upon the head,
It assures of union with Christ and Heaven that waits ahead.

Wield the Sword of Scripture at Satan when with him in fight,
And he will have no recourse but to take quick flight.

No armor for the back reveals the believer isn't to turn and run,
But faithfully fight the battle 'til Satan is defeated and the victory is won.

Each day for warfare the believer is to prepare
By putting on this armor in fervent prayer.

D.L. Moody was not fond of the hymn "Onward Christian Soldiers" and preferred his songleader Ira Sankey not to use it. Moody believed this song was not true to experience. He said, "The church is a poor army." "We indeed are "a poor army," because we do not use the equipment God has provided for us. God commands us to stand and withstand! And he enables us to do it!" (Wiersbe, The Strategy of Satan, 139)

"Fight the good fight." (1 Timothy 1:18) J.C. Ryle commented, "It is a fight of universal necessity. No rank or class or age can plead exemption, or escape the battle. Ministers and people, preachers and hearers, old and young, high and low, rich and poor, gentle and simple, kings and subjects, landlords and tenants, learned and unlearned—all alike must carry arms and go to war. All have by nature a heart full of pride, unbelief, sloth, worldliness and sin. All are living in a world beset with snares, traps and pitfalls for the soul. All have near them a busy, restless, malicious devil. All, from the queen in her palace down to the pauper in the workhouse, all must fight, if they would be saved.

It is a fight of perpetual necessity. It admits of no breathing time, no armistice, no truce. On weekdays as well as on Sundays, in private as well as in public, at home by the family fireside as well as abroad, in little things, like management of tongue and temper, as well as in great ones, like the government of kingdoms, the Christian's warfare must unceasingly go on. The foe we have to do with keeps no holidays never slumbers and never sleeps. So long as we have breath in our bodies, we must keep on our armor and remember we are on an enemy's ground. 'Even on the brink of Jordan,' said a dying saint, 'I find Satan nibbling at my heels.' We must fight until we die." (Ryle, "Holiness")

Max Lucado stated, "Even when Satan appears to win, he loses." (Lucado, For These Tough Times) Warren Wiersbe remarked, "As believers, we have this confidence: God is *always in complete control*. When God permits Satan to light the furnace, he always keeps his own hand on the thermostat!" (Wiersbe, The Strategy of Satan, 47) Stephen Olford wrote, "While Satan is a decided fact, a destructive force – praise the Lord, he is a defeated foe! As John the Apostle tells us, 'For this purpose the Son of God was manifested, that he might destroy the works of the devil.' (1 John 3:8) In the light of this, we can submit ourselves to God, resist the devil, and see him flee. (James 4:7)" (Taylor)

References on the doctrine of Satan
The Strategy of Satan, Warren W. Wiersbe
The Invisible War, Donald Grey Barnhouse
Victory over the Devil, Jack R. Taylor
How to Meet the Enemy, John MacArthur

Digging Deeper
1. What is Satan's purpose toward you?
2. How were Peter (Matthew 26:58, 69, 70); Demas (2 Timothy 4:10) and Thomas (John 20:27) shipwrecked by Satan?
3. The Gospel Armor is the believer's attire for spiritual battle. What are the seven pieces of armor the Christian is to put on daily that he may be victorious over the wiles of the devil?
4. How should the Gospel Armor be put on?

10

WITNESSING

"The other things we have to do may be called important by those around us, but there is nothing on earth more important to do than to win a person to Jesus Christ." Bailey Smith (Smith, Bailey 118)

"When preaching and private talk are not available, you need to have a tract ready. . . Get good striking tracts or none at all. But a touching gospel tract may be the seed of eternal life. Therefore, do not go out without your tracts." C.H. Spurgeon (Spurgeon, The Soulwinner, 172-173)

In Acts 1:8 Jesus exhorts all believers to be His "witnesses." A witness is one who tells the truth about something that he has experienced first hand. Jesus wants the saved to simply tell their story of salvation couched in the message and meaning of His death, burial and resurrection. (Matthew 10:32-33; I Peter 3:15) Years ago two families resided in Kentucky. One had the only radio for miles. This family heard that a tornado was heading straight for their neighbor's house so the father sent his son Merle to give warning. Merle darted out the door to do just that, but a bird landed on a limb and he stopped to throw a stone at it. He missed. He then started running to fulfill his mission again when the bird flew back to another limb close to him. This time his rock was right on target and the bird fell to the ground. As he picked up the bloody bird he heard a rushing sound coming from the direction of the Renfro family's home in the valley – the family he was to warn. He looked toward it just in time to see their four bodies thrust to death. He rushed back to tell his father what had happened. In the midst of the story his father noticed blood on his hands and asked him what that was. Merle told him it was the blood of the bird he killed. His father replied, "No, son that's not the blood of the bird you killed. It is the blood of the Renfro family you failed to warn." (Smith, Bailey 163-164) Most believers are guilty of throwing stones at birds while people all around them die and go to Hell, and their hands are wringing wet with their blood! Look at your hands. Do you see the blood of a friend, an acquaintance, a stranger, or a family member dripping from them? God states one day believers will be held accountable for those to whom they had the chance to witness and didn't. (Ezekiel 33: 7-9) That is unalterable.

R.A. Torrey declared, "I would like to ask what right a man has to call himself a follower of Jesus Christ if he is not a soul-winner? There is absolutely no such thing as following Christ unless you make the purpose of Christ's life the purpose of your life." (uncleernest.com)

The Christian should engage in witnessing in response to four calls.

The Call from above: Christ on His throne in Heaven calls the saved to be His witness. He declares, "Ye shall be witnesses unto me both in Jerusalem (home area) and in all Judea (state) and in Samaria (across America) and unto the uttermost parts of the earth" (everywhere else) (Acts 1:8); "I have chosen you, that you should go and bring forth fruit" (John 15:16); and "Follow me and I will make you fishers of men" (Matthew 4:19). Total baptisms in the Southern Baptist Convention are the lowest since 1970, revealing the neglect of soulwinning despite the Lord's crystal clear command *to go and tell.*

"We are a denomination that, for the most part, has lost its evangelistic passion." Thom Rainer (Rainer 6)

The Call from Around: Broken, bleeding, bound, and blind souls are crying out for help. Their body language and lifestyle are but a plea for you to tell them of Him who alone can make the eternal difference in their life.

The Call from Within: In the heart of the saved is the voice of the Holy Spirit pleading "Go and tell of Calvary's love and Jesus' desire to save from sin." Indeed, with Paul the saint cries, "The love of Christ constraineth me" to go and tell. God plants within the soul of all He saves the desire to reproduce. In fact the person who has no desire to tell is not "born of Him" (Matthew 10: 32-33). W.A. Criswell said, "The first impulse of a born-again Christian is to win somebody to Jesus. If we lose this drive, we are untrue to the Holy Spirit within us and we deny the great will of God for us." (Autrey 6) I can understand how a person may work hard at soulwinning never to win a soul (though highly unlikely), but I will never understand how a person who claims to know Christ could never witness. It just doesn't mesh with what scripture teaches. In the Bible record after record is given about how those who Jesus saved immediately began to go and tell. Among these were Philip, Andrew, and the woman at Jacob's Well. The saved cannot but speak out loud for their Savior. He places within the saved soul a "divine heartburn" for the lost. Do you hear this call from within the citadel of your own heart to go and tell?

The Call from Below: A call comes ringing loud and clear from the torment and darkness of Hell for the saved to be a witness. Luke 16 gives the record of a man who died and went to Hell. In verses 27-28 the man cries from Hell to Abraham in Heaven, "I pray thee therefore father, that thou wouldest send him to my father's house; for I have five brothers; that he may testify unto them, lest they also come to this place of torment." This man begged from Hell for someone on earth to warn his brothers lest they die in their sin and end up there with him. Do you hear such pleas from Hell begging you to witness to a son, a daughter, a spouse, or a friend? A passion for souls must overwhelm you or you will never be serious about soul winning.

"If we only lead one soul to Jesus Christ we may set a stream in motion that will flow when we are dead and gone." D.L. Moody (Moody, <u>Great Preaching on Soul Winning</u>, 234)

The Holy Spirit empowers, emboldens, and enables you for witnessing. (Acts 4: 31-32) It is He that will use you in communicating the gospel effectively with the unsaved.

METHODS OF WITNESSING

In *Soulwinning 101* I share 275 helps for winning the lost to Christ. I include here two of the simplest and most effective methods. Regardless of method utilized, it is essential to avoid religious jargon unfamiliar with unbelievers. William Faulkner referring to Ernest Hemingway remarked, "He has never been known to use a word that might send a reader to the dictionary." (<u>Encarta</u>) In regard to the gospel witness the Christian must endeavor to do the same.

Personal Testimony

One of the greatest methods of witnessing is the use of one's salvation testimony. A personal testimony should include five specific points and easily be shared in three to five minutes. Fine tune the story of your conversion in such simplicity that even "a cave man can understand it."

(1) My life before meeting Christ.
(2) How I came to realize my need of Christ.
(3) What I did to become a Christian.
(4) My life since I became a Christian.
(5) Appeal. Would you be willing to do as I and receive Jesus Christ into your life as Lord and Savior?

Colors of Salvation Card

This laminated card has the colors of salvation on one side and the explanation of each on the other. I have used it often with great effectiveness with all ages. This presentation could be adapted for use with the Wordless book and the Witnessing bracelet. This card is available through this ministry exclusively and is explained in detail in Soulwinning 101.

BLACK COLOR Black stands for man's sin against God that resulted in separation and condemnation. Sin is disobeying God. It is failure to keep His commandments. The Bible states, "All have sinned and fallen short of the glory of God." (Romans 3:23) All mankind is in the same boat spiritually and in need of a Savior. This sin has power to separate a person from God now and in eternity. The Bible in Romans 6:23 states, "The wages (consequences) of sin is death."

RED COLOR Red stands for the precious Blood of Jesus Christ that was shed at Calvary in response to man's desperate need and God's amazing love. John says, "The blood of Jesus

Christ cleanses from all sin." (I John 1:7) John 3:16 declares, "For God so loved the world (you) that He gave His only begotten son that whosoever (you) believes on Him should not perish but have everlasting life."

WHITE COLOR White stands for the soul's cleansing upon repentance and faith in Jesus Christ. The condition of salvation (forgiveness) is "repentance toward God and faith in the Lord Jesus Christ." (Acts 20:21) To repent is to change one's mind about both the sin of which he has committed and the place he gives God in life.

BLUE COLOR Blue stands for one's confession of Christ openly in believer's baptism. Baptism does not save a person; one is baptized because of salvation. (Matthew 10:32-33)

GREEN COLOR Green stands for the disciplines essential for spiritual growth. Once a person receives Christ as Savior and Lord he is as a "newborn babe" requiring help to "grow up" in Christ Jesus. Scripture urges the believer to "grow in the grace and knowledge of our Lord and Savior Jesus Christ." (II Peter 3:18)

PURPLE COLOR Purple stands for the Lordship of Christ in the believer's life. Jesus is to be "Lord of all." Acts 10:36 states, "The word which *God* sent unto the children of Israel, preaching peace by Jesus Christ (he is Lord of all)."

YELLOW COLOR Yellow stands for the saint's faithful service to Jesus Christ. Christians are to be "faithful unto death" in service and stand. John admonishes, "Fear none of those things which thou shalt suffer: behold, the devil shall cast *some* of you into prison, that ye may be tried; and ye shall have tribulation ten days: be thou faithful unto death, and I will give thee a crown of life." (Revelation 2:10)

GOLD COLOR <u>Gold</u> stands for the believer's eternal home in Heaven. Heaven awaits the child of God at the end of life's journey. Jesus in speaking of Heaven said, " In my Father's house are many mansions: if *it were* not *so*, I would have told you. I go to prepare a place for you. And if I go and prepare a place for you, I will come again, and receive you unto myself; that where I am, *there* ye may be also." (John 14:1–3)

GRAY COLOR <u>Gray</u> stands for the Valley of Decision in which the unsaved reside. The prophet Joel cried "Multitudes, multitudes in the valley of decision in the day of the Lord." (Joel 3:14) The Lord calls on man to make a decision concerning personal sin and his relationship to Him.

In a day when nearly 6000 die every hour without Christ be busy about telling others about their need of being "Born Again." You may be a friend's only roadblock on the road to Hell. Brazen up and tell of Jesus to them before it's too late. Friends don't let friends die and go to Hell.

Jacques Lefevre, evangelist of the Swiss Reformation, prayed, "When will Christ be all in all? When will the only study, the only consolation, the only desire of all be to know the Gospel, to cause it to advance everywhere, and to be firmly persuaded, as our ancestors, of this primitive church, dyed by the blood of martyrs, who understood that knowing nothing, except the Gospel, is to know everything." (Johnston 419)

C.H. Spurgeon on his salvation
"Believer, do you recollect the day when your fetters fell off? Do you remember the place when Jesus met you, and said, 'I have loved thee with an everlasting love; I have blotted out as a cloud thy transgressions, and as a thick cloud thy sins; they shall not be mentioned against thee any more

for ever.' Oh! what a sweet season is that when Jesus takes away the pain of sin. When the Lord first pardoned my sin, I was so joyous that I could scarce refrain from dancing. I thought on my road home from the house where I had been set at liberty, that I must tell the stones in the street the story of my deliverance. So full was my soul of joy, that I wanted to tell every snow-flake that was falling from heaven of the wondrous love of Jesus, who had blotted out the sins of one of the chief of rebels. But it is not only at the commencement of the Christian life that believers have reason for song; as long as they live they discover cause to sing in the ways of the Lord, and their experience of his constant loving kindness leads them to say, 'I will bless the Lord at all times: his praise shall continually be in my mouth.'" (Spurgeon, Morning, February 1)

References on Soulwinning
The Soulwinner, C.H. Spurgeon
Words to Winners of Souls, Horatius Bonar
How to Give Away Your Faith, Paul Little
The Master's Plan of Evangelism, Robert E. Coleman
Drawing the Net, O.S. Hawkins
Soulwinning 101 (275 Helps for the Soulwinner), Frank Shivers

Digging Deeper
1. What is the meaning of the term 'witness?'
2. Relate the story of the failed warning by Merle. How does that relate to witnessing?
3. In what ways can Phillip's witnessing encounter with the Eunuch teach one how to share their faith?
4. Who enables the Christian to be an effective witness?

5. What is the five-point presentation of a personal testimony? Share your testimony based upon these five points with the class, friend or family member.
6. What are the "Colors of Salvation" and their meaning

11

40 WORDS EVERY CHRISTIAN SHOULD UNDERSTAND

A n understanding of some basic words of the Bible and the Church is greatly beneficial to the child of God. In this chapter, forty key words will be defined with relevant scripture passages cited.

Adoption

Spiritual adoption is the divinely decreed "Sonship" of a sinner into the family of God through the New Birth. (Romans 8:15; Galatians 4:5) A person, though an outcast and enemy to God, through the New Birth is brought into His family with the full benefits and blessings presently and eternally that belong to His Son (1 John 3: 1) and receive the nature of His Son. (2 Corinthians 5:21)

Amen

Expression of hearty approval. (I Chronicles 16:36)

Antichrist

The final great opponent of Christ; a rival Christ who will be revealed at the start of the Great Tribulation. This title is only found in John's epistles. (1 John 2:18)

Armageddon

Literally means "Mount of Megiddo," a small mountain that overlooks the Mediterranean Sea. It is in this valley that Joel prophecies that a war like none other will occur between the forces of righteousness (God) and Satan in the end time. (Joel 3:12; Revelation 16:16)

Atonement

At-one-ment, the state of being reconciled to God by means of Jesus' death, burial and resurrection. (Romans 5:11) Man in his inherit state is alienated from God by sin. (Colossians 1:21; Ephesians 2:12) Jesus Christ bridges the chasm of separation for all who receive Him as Lord and Savior making them right with God. (1 Timothy 2:5)

Born Again

Spiritual re-birth, not physical, that occurs at the moment a sinner confesses Jesus as Lord and Savior exhibiting repentance and faith. (Acts 20:21; John 3:3; I Peter 1:23) It results in a radical change in conscience, conduct and conviction. (2 Corinthians 5:17)

Carnal

This is a Christian who lives under the control of the "flesh" and its sensual appetites instead of in the fullness of the Holy Spirit. A Worldly Christian. (Romans 8: 5-7; 1 Corinthians 3: 1-3-4)

Church

The church is primarily the local assembly of baptized believers in Jesus Christ. (Acts 5:42) The Greek word for church is *ekklesia* which means "the called out ones" or "assembly." Refer to Chapter Three for further explanation.

Christian

This term is greatly misused when referring to one's culture, church, religious upbringing or belief. In reality, it means to belong to Christ and to have a personal relationship with Christ as Lord and Savior. Believers were first called Christians in Antioch. (Acts 11:26)

Confession

(1) The acknowledgement of sin. (1 John 1:9; Ezra 10:11) Following his adultery, David confessed his sin unto God, pleading for forgiveness and restoration. (Psalm 51: 1-4) (2) The declaration of one's Christian convictions and beliefs. (Romans 1:16; Matthew 10: 32-33)

Covenant

A binding agreement or contract between God and man. It may be conditional or unconditional. There are eight important covenants in the Bible; Salvation covenant with man (Titus 1:1-2; Hebrews 13:20); Covenant with Adam (Genesis 1:28; 2:15-15; 3:15-19); Covenant with Noah (Genesis 8:21-22); Covenant with Abraham (Genesis 12: 2-3, 7; 13:14-17; 15:5,18; 17:8); Covenant with Moses and Israel (Exodus 19: 3-8; Leviticus 26; Deuteronomy 28); Covenant with David (2 Chronicles 13:5; 2 Samuel 7:12-16; 23:5); Covenant with the Church (Matthew 16:18; 26:28; Luke 22:20; Hebrews 13: 20-21) and the New Covenant with Israel (Jeremiah 31:31-34; Isaiah 42:6; Isaiah 43:1-6; Deuteronomy 1:1-9; Hebrews 8:7-12).

Demons

Evil spirits (fallen angels) who are the servants of Satan. There is one Devil and many demons. (Ephesians 6:12) Demons may "oppress" the saint but cannot "possess" the saint.

Depravity

Corruption, immorality, wickedness of man at the core of his being necessitating Divine intervention and remedy. (Romans 7:18)

Eternal Security

The true believer is eternally saved. (John 6:37) John MacArthur commented on Jude 1, "That phrase can be translated in the dative or the instrumental case. I prefer the latter, which would render the word 'in' as 'by,' reading 'kept by Jesus Christ.' The Greek verb is tereo, which means 'to watch, stand guard over, or keep.' It stresses a watchful care to guard something as cherished as a priceless treasure. Do you know how secure I am? Just as secure as the power of the Lord Jesus Christ who keeps me. That is a fantastic concept! This keeping is permanent." (MacArthur "Beware") See Chapter One for further explanation of eternal security.

Faith

To exhibit trust in and reliance upon God and all He says. (Hebrews 11:1, 6; Ephesians 2: 8-9) Martin Luther stated, "Faith is a living and unshakable confidence, a belief in God so assured that a man would die a thousand deaths for its sake." (Johnson) John Trapp remarked, "It is the nature of faith to believe God upon His bare word.... It will not be, saith sense; it cannot be, saith reason; it both can and will be, saith faith, for I have a promise." (realmoffaith.org) Manley Beasley defined faith, "Faith is acting as though a thing is so when it is not so, in order for it to be so, because it is so." D.L. Moody stated, "Faith does not look within; it looks without. It is not what I think, or what I feel, or what I have done, but it is what Jesus Christ is and has done." (Moody, The D.L. Moody Book, 33) John Paton, missionary for the South Sea islanders, translated the Scriptures and hit a brick wall in coming up with a word that conveyed the concept of faith, trust or believing. One day a native came running into Paton's study, flopped down due to exhaustion and said, "It feels so good to rest my whole weight in this chair." Paton had his translation. "Faith is resting your whole weight on God." This definition helped bring a whole civilization to Christ. (MacArthur, How to Meet, 111) "Trust is believing Jesus can, Faith is believing Jesus will."

Glorification

The state of perfection, total conformity to the image of Christ that occurs at the final resurrection. (Philippians 3:21; 1 John 3:2) I await heaven not primarily for relief from trials nor reunion with saints but release from this body of flesh (corruption) that often disappoints God due to sin.

Grace

The unmerited favor of God (clemency, kindness) toward man in salvation demonstrated through His son Jesus Christ at Calvary. (Ephesians 2: 8 -9) An acrostic of Grace defines Grace as God's Riches At Christ's Expense. Grace is not confined to salvation because it continues its work in making possible forgiveness and change in the believer's life by the power of God.

Hallelujah

The expression of joy, praise or thanks unto God. Literally (Hebrew) it means "Praise the Lord." (Psalms 146) Greek version (NT) is *Alleluia*. (Revelation 19:1) Augustine said that a Christian ought to be a "Hallelujah" from the sole of his feet to the crown of his head. The Christian as he lifts up one foot should shout "Hallelujah" and then as he brings it down shout "Praise the Lord."

Holiness

"Holiness is the habit of being of one mind with God, according as we find His mind described in Scripture. It is the habit of agreeing in God's judgment; hating what He hates, loving what He loves, and measuring everything in this world by the standard of His Word. He who most entirely agrees with God, he is the most holy man." (Ryle, "Holiness") Holiness involves separation from all that contaminates and defiles. (Matthew 5:8; Romans 12:1; 1 Thessalonians 4:7; Hebrews 12:14)

Hypocrisy

The acts of preaching or declaring one thing regarding belief and conduct while practicing another intentionally; "mask wearing" as in theatrical performances leading others to believe a person is someone he is not. Jesus strongly condemns hypocrisy in the church. (Luke 6:42; Matthew 15:7-8) D. L. Moody said hypocrisy was "talking cream and living skim milk." (Newell 469)

Infallibility (Inerrancy)

The Bible is free from the liability to mislead, deceive, or err. (Psalm 12:6) The Bible is unmixed with errors in its original writing (Autograph Copy). Man's rejection or neglect of Holy Scripture does not alter its power to accomplish God's purposes. (Isaiah 55:11) John R. Rice cautioned, "Do not study the Bible with the counsel of the enemies of the Bible. The liberal who would take the crown of deity from the head of the Son of God, who would trample underfoot the atoning blood of the Savior and who would take up the sneering question of Satan, "Yea, hath God said…?" is no fit teacher of God's Word. Jesus said about those who did not believe the Bible: "O fools, and slow of heart to believe all that the prophets have spoken" (Luke 24:25). The evidence that the Bible is the very infallible Word of God is overwhelming. So to listen to infidels is wrong." (Rice Viii)

Inheritance
Believers are "joint heirs" with Christ Jesus by divine relationship inheriting every possession that belongs to Him. (Romans 8:17; Hebrews 1:2; 2 Peter 1:3-4; 2 Corinthians 1:20; Ephesians 1: 11-12) Spurgeon said, "Even if I should say all that I could upon all these texts (passages about inheritance and adoption) put together, I should not then have said as much as this text (Romans 8:17) says." (Spurgeon "Heirs of God") Spurgeon was remarking that Romans 8:17 was over the top, that nothing really else needed to be said regarding the saints inheritance. The believer is "heir of God", all else included in the believer's inheritance (permanence, peace, position, provision, promises) pales in light of this fact.

Inspiration
Inspiration as used in 2 Timothy 3:16 does not mean that scripture is inspiring to read, though it is, but that it is divinely "breathed out" of the heart of God; originated in its totality with God. (Matthew 4:4; Luke 4:4)

Justification
The act of God by which He wipes clean the slate of man's sin (pardons) and satisfies the claims of the law through the saving work of His son Jesus Christ. Justification for the believer means *Just-as-if-I-never sinned* (Romans 4:25); to be forgiven of all sin and completely acquitted of all offenses as if they never occurred. (Romans 8:1; Romans 5:1-11)

Mercy

(1.) The compassion, loving-kindness, pity and goodness expressed by God for the sinner and their condemned plight. (Ephesians 2:4; Romans 11:30-32) (2.) The pity, compassion, and love of God expressed to believers in times of spiritual failure. (Psalm 51:1; 103:8-11) (3.) Christians are to exhibit mercy to those who sin and repent. (Matthew 5:7) C.H. Spurgeon exhorts, "Mercies should be remembered. It is a great wrong to God when we bury his mercies in the grave of unthankfulness. Especially is this the case with distinguishing mercies, wherein the Lord makes us to differ from others. Light, when the rest of the land is in darkness! Life, when others are smitten with the sword of death! Liberty from an iron bondage! O Christians, these are not things to be forgotten! Abundantly utter the memory of distinguishing mercies! Discriminating grace deserves unceasing memorials of praise. Mercies multiplied should never be forgotten. If they are new every morning, our memory of them should be always fresh." (Spurgeon "Sin")

Messiah

Anointed One sent from God; Jesus Christ the Christ. Christ means *Messiah*. (John 1:41; 4:35) Jesus means *Savior.* (Matthew 1:21)

Millennium

A period of 1000 years in which Jesus with His saints will reign on earth and Satan will be bound. (Revelation 20:7; Zechariah 14:4-5, 9)

New Birth

Synonymous with one being *Born Again*. See "Born Again".

Prophecy

The prediction or forth telling of a divine event prompted and governed by the Holy Spirit. (2 Peter 1:21; Revelation 22: 18-19) *Prophets.* John Stott stated, "We should certainly reject any claim that there are prophets today comparable to the biblical prophets. For they were the 'mouth' of God, special organs of revelation, whose teaching belongs to the foundation on which the church is built." (Stott, The Contemporary Christian, 104)

Rapture

"Caught up", the bodily transport of believers to Heaven at Christ's second coming. (1 Thessalonians 4: 14-17)

Regeneration

A change of being, a passing from death unto life brought about by the work of the Holy Spirit, literally "The New Birth." (John 1: 12 – 13)

Repentance

The change of mind, belief, direction toward God based upon "godly sorrow." It is to make a spiritual "about face." (Acts 20:21; 2 Corinthians 7:10) Repentance brings joy in heaven. (Luke 15:7)

Resurrection

The rising from death to life, not resuscitation of Jesus Christ (Acts 4:33) and at the end of the age the raising of all the saints. (1 Corinthians 15: 35 – 57)

Sanctification

Essentially it means to appoint or set apart for a holy or special purpose. (1 Corinthians 1:2; Hebrews 10:10) Believers are divinely 'set apart' at conversion and enabled to progress in sanctification by the power of God. (1 Peter

1:15-16; 2 Chronicles 29:5; Proverbs 4:18; 2 Corinthians 7:1) C.H. Spurgeon remarks, "Sanctification is the work of God's Spirit (2 Thessalonians 2:13), whereby we are renewed in the whole man after the image of God (Ephesians 4:24), and are enabled more and more to die to sin, and live to righteousness (Romans 6:11)." (Spurgeon, Puritan Catechism) Ray C. Steadman commented, "Sanctification is the process by which the inner worth which God imparts to our human spirit by faith in Christ begins to work itself out into our conduct. We actually begin to change. We begin to be like what we actually are. Therefore, our attitudes change, and our actions change, and our habits begin to change, and we stop certain things and begin others. Our whole demeanor is different; we become much more gracious, happy, wholesome persons. That is called sanctification..." (Steadman, "If God")

Salvation

Salvation is the state of deliverance in a sinner's life from the penalty, power and, in Heaven, even the presence of sin by the divine intervention of God through His son Jesus Christ. (Acts 4:12; Titus 2:11) "Salvation is a good word; it denotes that comprehensive purpose of God by which he justifies, sanctifies, and glorifies his people: first pardoning their offences and accepting them as righteous in his sight; then progressively transforming them by his Spirit into the image of Christ, until finally they become like Christ in heaven, when they see him as he is, and their bodies are raised incorruptible like Christ's body of glory." (Stevenson 51)

Sin

The transgression (violation) of the Law of God, acts of defilement and defiance. (I John 3:4) All have sinned. (Romans 3:23; 1 John 1: 8, 10) C.H. Spurgeon remarked,

"One sin can ruin a soul for ever; it is not in the power of the human mind to grasp the infinity of evil that slumbereth in the bowels of one solitary sin." (Spurgeon, "Particular Redemption")

Spiritual Gifts

Gifts bestowed to believers by the Holy Spirit at conversion that vary from believer to believer. (Romans 12:6-8; 1 Corinthians 12:8-10; 12:28; 12:29-30)

Temptation

(1) An enticement or lure to do evil. Satan and his demons tempt all mankind to disobey God. God tempts no man to evil. (James 1: 12-15) Deliverance from temptation is possible. (1 Corinthians 10:31; Matthew 6:13) (2) A time of testing from God to prove devotion and commitment while strengthening the saint's faith. (Genesis 22: 1-19; Job 1 – 2; 1 Peter 1: 3-9)

Tribulation

(1)The oppression and persecution believers confront in living for Christ. (2 Thessalonians 3:4) (2) The Tribulation is a seven-year period of suffering and persecution under the reign of the Antichrist that follows the rapture of the church. (Revelation 7:14; Matthew 24: 21-22; 2 Thessalonians 2: 8-9) The final three and a half years of this period is called *The Great Tribulation.*

Trinity

Term used to describe that God is a unity of three persons: God the Father, God the Son, and God the Holy Spirit. (Matthew 28:19)

Digging Deeper
1. What does it mean for a person to be "adopted" into the family of God?
2. Who are Christians?
3 What is meant by the term "infallibility" as it relates to the Bible?
4. Define the term "justification."
5. What is meant by the term "rapture" as it relates to the second coming of Christ?
6. Define the term "trinity."
7. What is "grace?"
8. How does Martin Luther define "faith?"
9. How would you defend the position, "Once saved, always saved?"

12

OVERVIEW OF THE BIBLE

The word for Bible (*Biblia*) means books. The Bible is a divine compilation of books regarding God's acts and communication with man. The Bible consists of 66 Books and is divided into two divisions, the Old Testament and New Testament. There was no Old Testament and New Testament prior to Christ's coming, only one body of Holy Scripture. The word "Testament" is best rendered *covenant,* an agreement or promise between God and man. The Old Testament is God's covenant with man about salvation prior to Christ's coming. The New Testament is God's covenant with man about salvation in Christ Jesus. The Old Testament covenant has to do with Mt. Sinai (Law); the New Testament covenant has to do with Mt. Calvary (Grace). The Old Testament records the preparation made for the coming of Jesus while the New Testament has to do with His arrival, life, works, death, burial and resurrection for the redemption of mankind.

John Stott stated, "The Bible is essentially a handbook of salvation. Its overarching purpose is to teach not facts of science (e.g. the nature of moon rock) which men can discover by their own empirical investigation, but facts of salvation, which no space exploration can discover but only

God can reveal. The whole Bible unfolds the divine scheme of salvation - man's creation in God's image, his fall through disobedience into sin and under judgment, God's continuing love for him in spite of his rebellion, God's eternal plan to save him through his covenant of grace with a chosen people, culminating in Christ; the coming of Christ as the Savior, who died to bear man's sin, was raised from death, was exalted to heaven and sent the Holy Spirit; and man's rescue first from guilt and alienation, then from bondage, and finally from mortality in his progressive experience of the liberty of God's children." (Stott, The Message of 2 Timothy, 102)

The New Testament is named for its subject matter of the new declaration of God's will in His son Jesus Christ and new covenant of grace. (Jeremiah 31: 31 -34; 1 Corinthians 11:25; 2 Corinthians 3:6; Hebrews 8:8-13; 9:15; 12:24) Regarding the Old Testament name the Apostle Paul refers to it as such in 1 Corinthians 3:14.

Old Testament

The Old Testament is comprised of 39 books and is divided into five categories.

Pentateuch
Genesis, Exodus, Leviticus, Numbers, Deuteronomy

Historical Books
Joshua, Judges, Ruth, First and Second Samuel, First and Second Kings, First and Second Chronicles, Ezra, Nehemiah, Esther

Poetic
Job, Psalms, Proverbs, Ecclesiastes, Song of Solomon

Prophetic (Two Categories)
(1) Major Prophets
Isaiah, Jeremiah, Lamentations, Ezekiel, Daniel
(2) Minor Prophets
Hosea, Joel, Amos, Obadiah, Jonah, Micah, Nahum, Habakkuk, Zephaniah, Haggai, Zechariah, Malachi

New Testament
    The New Testament consists of 27 books and may be divided into five categories.

The Four Gospels
Matthew, Mark, Luke, John

The Pauline Epistles
Romans, First and Second Corinthians, Galatians, Ephesians, Philippians, Colossians, First and Second Thessalonians, First and Second Timothy, Titus, Philemon

History
Acts of the Apostles

The General Epistles
Hebrews, James, First and Second Peter, First, Second and Third John, Jude

Book on Last Things
Revelation

Synopsis of Bible Books

Old Testament
    Genesis. Creation; the flood of Judgment; Israel's enslavement.

Exodus. Plagues, Moses leads the Israelites out of captivity, Ten Commandments, Blue-prints for Tabernacle.

Leviticus. The ceremonial law and the revelation of Christ in the law.

Numbers. 40-year wilderness wanderings begin and murmurings of the Israelites.

Deuteronomy. The law rehearsed; the death of Moses.

Joshua. The minority report to trust God to enter the Promised Land and possess it.

Judges. A time of "no King" but of 13 Judges. Judges 2: 16- 19 capsules Israel history at this time.

Ruth. The story of Naomi, Ruth and Boaz.

First & Second Samuel. Story of the reigns of Saul and David. Record of David's adultery and murder of Uriah the Hittite.

First & Second Kings. A record of the reign of the Jewish Kings who ruled Israel. What began as one nation eventually divided into two.

First & Second Chronicles. A record of the Kings and genealogy with encouragement to rebuild the Temple.

Ezra. The story of the return of the Jews from the Babylonian captivity.

Nehemiah. Nehemiah's leadership in the rebuilding of the walls about Jerusalem and reinstitution of worship despite grave opposition. A time of revival.

Esther. Queen Esther intervenes in behalf of the Jews and saves them from a holocaust. God's name does not appear in any variation.

Job. Satan tempts a righteous and Godly man in Edom without success. A narrative of one man's patience, endurance and faith despite grave suffering and calamity.

Psalms. The hymnbook of the Bible comprised mostly of David's songs of praise and adoration to God for His many deliverances and provisions.

Proverbs. Wise instructions on living ethically, morally and spiritually.

Ecclesiastes. An empty man's search for meaning and significance.

Song of Solomon. A love song between Christ and His Church.

Isaiah. Isaiah prophesied some 700 years before Christ about the Messiah's coming. Proclaims God's judgment on Judah.

Jeremiah. The 'weeping prophet'. Jeremiah grieved over Judah's moral and spiritual decay.

Lamentations. Jeremiah's sorrow over Israel's calamity.

Ezekiel. God's glory and the honor of His name.

Daniel. Story of Daniel, the man who would not bow to compromise and major prophecies concerning Christ.

Hosea. The marriage of Hosea and Gomer illustrates the redeeming love of God for a wayward people.

Joel. A call to repentance. Uses the imagery of locusts regarding judgment.

Amos. Pronouncement of judgment upon Israel, rejection of God's warning.

Obadiah. Announcement of the doom of Edom.

Jonah. The story of Jonah the fugitive fleeing from God who finally becomes the first foreign missionary. Revival in Nineveh and the city is spared judgment.

Micah. God expects man to "to do justly, and to love mercy" and live obediently. Prophesizes the birth place of the Son of God.

Nahum. Proclaims the destruction of Nineveh (125 years after Jonah).

Habakkuk. The victory of faith over difficulty. "The just shall live by faith."

Zephaniah. Preached judgment in the midst of a false revival.

Haggai. The House of God sat uncompleted. Haggai's bold preaching got the people back to work again.

Zechariah. The re-building of the Temple and messianic prophecies.

Malachi. The backsliding of Israel and the priests; a bold pronouncement against it.

New Testament

Gospel of Matthew. Jesus is presented as Teacher and the promised Messiah of the Old Testament. Genealogy of Jesus through Joseph.

Gospel of Mark. Life and works of Jesus the Messiah. Pictures Jesus as a servant. About a third of Mark deals with the last week of Jesus' life.

Gospel of Luke. The compassionate Christ, the Savior of all. Genealogy of Jesus through Mary. Largest volume of the gospels.

Gospel of John. Presents the person and work of Christ as the Son of God and His acts and discourses that are not recorded elsewhere. The "salvation textbook."

Acts of the Apostles. Acts of the Holy Spirit through the church in evangelism, how the Gospel spread throughout the world. Paul's missionary journeys.

Epistle to the Romans. Doctrine of salvation (justification by faith) coupled with duties of the Christian life.

First Epistle to the Corinthians. A letter of correction and direction to a 'Troubled Church.' Abuse of the Lord's Supper and the matter of lawsuits.

Second Epistle to the Corinthians. Help for a 'Troubled Church' part 2; Paul gives defense of his authority as an apostle.

Epistle to the Galatians. Christian liberty, freedom by God's grace, repudiation of legalism.

Epistle to the Ephesians. Christian living, the believer's position in Christ Jesus.

Epistle to the Philippians. The Christian's joy and message.

Epistle to the Colossians. A letter of rebuke regarding false teaching in the church at Colossi. The apostle Paul writes to establish saints soundly in the Truth.

First Epistle to the Thessalonians. Last Things (Second Coming of Christ) and teaching on purity.

Second Epistle to the Thessalonians. Last Things. The Apostle Paul corrects an error regarding the coming of the Lord.

First Timothy. Ministerial instruction to pastors and how all should conduct themselves in the church. Requirement for deacons.

Second Timothy. The Apostle Paul's swan song to Timothy; final instruction, warning and encouragement to his "son in the faith."

Epistle to Titus. The Apostle Paul instructs the pastor Titus; people are to practice what they profess.

Epistle to Philemon. A moving narrative of a runaway slave who gets saved and returns to his legal owner who is a Christian. "For love's sake."

Epistle to the Hebrews. Christ 'Above All'; "Better than" the angels, prophets, the Leviticial priests, etc.

Epistle of James. "Faith without works is dead." Live like a believer.

First Peter. Encouraging words to suffering saints. Mentions baptism.

Second Peter. Warning about false doctrine; insights about the Lord's return.

First Epistle of John. Birthmarks of the true believer, the conduct of a child of God.

Second Epistle of John. Stay loyal to the truth of God, always walk in the love of God.

Third Epistle of John. No person should be like Diotrephes who loves to have pre-eminence in the church; the saints should serve together in love.

Epistle of Jude. Warnings of false teachers and appeal for the saints to contend earnestly for the faith.

The Revelation. The commendation and condemnation of the seven churches; the future of the church revealed. Christ's ultimate conquest.

References on the Bible

What the Bible is all About, Henrietta Mears

Nelson's Quick Reference Bible Commentary, Warren W. Wiersbe

Halley's Handbook on the Bible, Henry H. Halley

Digging Deeper

1. What are the five categories of books in the Old Testament?
2. What books are classified as "poetic?"
3. What books are classified as "prophetic?"
4. What are the five categories of books in the New Testament?
5. Name the "Pauline epistles."
6. What is the book of "last things?"
7. Define the word "testament."
8. Why are the Old Testament and New Testament so named?
9. What New Testament book is considered "The Salvation Book?"

13

THE "NEGLECT NOT'S" OF GROWTH

The Bible is complete with many "Neglect Not's" of spiritual growth for the Christian's attention and obedience. The reason a Christian stumbles in his walk with the Lord is due to neglecting one or more of these "Neglect Not's." A person just cannot neglect something God exhorts to "Neglect Not" and expect to soar spiritually. In completing this study consider several essential "Neglect Not's" of Christian growth.

NEGLECT NOT SALVATION

This first "neglect not" of the Bible is foundational to the observance of the rest. The writer of Hebrews exhorted "Neglect not so great salvation" because in doing so "How shall you escape" its dreadful consequences? (Hebrews 2:3) Perhaps you have pondered a decision for Jesus Christ in this study but to this point you have neglected making it. Desist in this delay now and show "repentance toward God and faith in the Lord Jesus Christ" (Acts 20:21) James wrote, "What is your life? It's but a vapor that appeareth for a little time and then passeth away". (James 4:14) This door of opportunity to be saved is wide open presently, but it can shut quickly without warning. I press to your heart the question of this text, "How shall you escape?" If you neglect this great salvation of God through His son Jesus Christ, how do you expect to escape a wasted life, a wasted influence, emptiness and meaninglessness, and eternal damnation in Hell? What is your answer? It cannot be answered, can it? There is no way to escape these things apart from a relationship with the Lord Jesus Christ. *Neglect Not* this great invitation to be saved from a gracious Lord any longer. Join the family of God now by receiving Jesus as Lord and Savior.

The scapegoat in the Old Testament is a shadow of Christ. The high priest on the Day of Atonement would place his hands upon the head of a goat that was without spot or blemish and confess the sin of the people, symbolically transferring their sin. This scapegoat (sin-bearer) of the people would be led by a chosen man into the desert to be let loose where it could never be found. (Leviticus 16: 20-22) The Old Testament scapegoat pictures New Testament Atonement. Jesus Christ is the Supreme Scapegoat, provided by God to actually forgive sin and bear it into the "desert" of everlasting forgetfulness. Horatius Bonar said it so well,

> My sins were laid on Jesus,
> The spotless Lamb of God;
> He bore them all and freed me
> From the accursed load.
> My guilt was borne by Jesus;
> He cleansed the crimson stains
> In His own blood most precious
> And not a spot remains.

Max Lucado wrote, "It is possible to learn much about God's invitation and never respond to it personally. Yet his invitation is clear and nonnegotiable. He gives all and we give him all. Simple and absolute. He is clear in what he asks and clear in what he offers. The choice is up to us. Isn't it incredible that God leaves the choice to us? Think about it. There are many things in life we can't choose. We can't, for example, choose the weather. We can't control the economy. We can't choose whether or not we are born with a big nose or blue eyes or a lot of hair. We can't even choose how people respond to us. But we can choose where we spend eternity. The big choice, God leaves to us. The critical decision is ours. What are you doing with God's invitation?" (Lucado, And the Angels were Silent, 85)

In faith, confess and repent of sin, and trust Jesus to save and He will. Here and now pray:

"Lord Jesus, thank you for dying upon the Cross and being raised from the dead to make possible the forgiveness of sin. I stand in need of cleansing and forgiveness that I may be made right with God. I am sorry for my sin and desire to turn from it to live alone for you. I receive you now, Jesus, into my life as Lord and Savior. Amen."

NEGLECT NOT SCRIPTURE

Jesus admonished, "Search the scripture: for in them ye think ye have eternal life and they are they that testify of me." (John 5:39) This word "search" means to investigate, to examine, and to find out something, and it is an emphatic command of our Lord. Regarding searching, have you been obedient to this command or guilty of neglect? The writer of Hebrews states, "For the Word of God is quick, and powerful and sharper than a two-edged sword, piercing even to the dividing asunder of soul and spirit and of the joints and marrow and is a discerner of the thoughts and intents of the heart." (Hebrews 4:12) The Apostle Paul told young Timothy, "All scripture is given by inspiration of God and is profitable for doctrine, for reproof, for correction, for instruction in righteousness that the Man of God may be perfect, thoroughly furnished unto all good works." (2 Timothy 3:16-17) C.H. Spurgeon remarked, "No Scripture is exhausted by a single explanation. The flowers of God's garden bloom not only double, but sevenfold; they are continually pouring forth fresh fragrance." (D.L. Moody Yearbook 223)

Years ago in Uganda the native Christians would journey through high grass to a place of solitude daily to meet with God. It was apparent when someone failed to meet with God for a few days due to grass growing up on this path. Concerned saints would approach these Christians saying, "Brother, there is grass growing up on your path." How about you? Is there grass growing upon your path to solitude with God in His Word? Have you neglected Holy Scripture? Have you allowed pleasure or people to keep you from it? The Bereans "searched the scripture daily" (Acts 17:11), refusing to let grass grow upon their path to intimacy with the Almighty. Determine to be of the same mind, neglecting not the *intake* of mega scripture doses daily.

NEGLECT NOT SUPPLICATION

Jesus declared, "Men ought to always pray and not faint." (Luke 18:1) David testified, "When *thou* saith, Seek my face; my heart said unto thee, Thy face, Lord, will I seek." (Psalm 27:8) Pray when you feel like it, when you don't feel like it, until you do feel like it. Martyn Lloyd Jones stated, "Always respond to every impulse to pray. The impulse to pray may come when you are reading or when you are battling with a text. I would make an absolute law of this – always obey such an impulse." (Prayer and Intercession Quotes) John Bunyan exhorted, "Pray often, for prayer is a shield to the soul, a sacrifice to God, and a scourge for Satan." (Prayer and Intercession Quotes) François Fénelon declared, "Of all the duties enjoined by Christianity none is more essential and yet more neglected than prayer." (Prayer and Intercession Quotes) C.H. Spurgeon remarked, "There is a general kind of praying which fails for lack of precision. It is as if a regiment of soldiers should all fire off their guns anywhere. Possibly somebody would be killed, but the majority of the enemy would be missed." (Spurgeon, Sermons, 21) David Jeremiah expanded Spurgeon's comment and stated, "How often have we prayed something like, 'O Lord, be with cousin Billy now in a special way'? Have we stopped to consider what it is we're requesting? Imagine that you are a parent who is preparing to leave your children with a baby-sitter. Would you dream of saying, 'O, Betsy, I ask you now that you would be with my children in a special way?' No way. You would say, 'Betsy, the kids need to be in bed by 9 p.m. They can have one snack before their baths, and please make sure they finish their homework. You can reach us at this number if there's any problem. Any questions before we go?' We are very specific with our requests and instructions for our babysitters. We want them to know specifics. It should be no different with prayer." (Prayer and Intercession Quotes) Corrie Ten Boone sounded a striking note about the results of neglected prayer, stating, "When a Christian shuns fellowship with other Christians, the devil smiles. When he stops studying the Bible, the devil laughs. When he stops praying, the devil shouts for joy." (Prayer and Intercession Quotes) Pray, Pray, Pray dear believer.

C.H. Spurgeon declared, "Groans that words cannot express (Romans 8:26) are often prayers that God cannot refuse." (Cowman 486)

NEGLECT NOT THE SANCTUARY

In Hebrews believers are exhorted, "Do not forsake the assembling of yourselves together as the manner of some is, but exhort one another; and so much the more as ye see the day approaching." (Hebrews 10:25) Don't abandon or desert the church but stay integrally involved in the church. One's life or ministry will not count for much outside the church. In times of spiritual coldness and indifference attend church because it is ever used by God to reach and reclaim His erring children.

NEGLECT NOT SOULWINNING

Jesus said, "But ye shall receive power, after that the Holy Ghost is come upon you; and ye shall be witnesses unto me both in Jerusalem, and in all Judea, and in Samaria and unto the uttermost part of the earth." (Acts 1:8) Jesus is clearly stating, "Do not neglect witnessing." Sadly, however, 92 percent of Southern Baptists do! I was on my way to preach and noticed the words on a pontoon boat that read, "Go" (on the left pontoon) and "Fish" (on the right pontoon). I challenge you to "Go Fish." Go fishing for souls in the fishpond of your campus, neighborhood, dormitory, job and neighborhood. Jesus didn't call "wise" those who preached, sang, or taught but said, "He that winneth souls is wise." (Proverbs 11:30) Speak out loud for Christ in the solitude or multitude; in the daylight or twilight; in the bliss of life or the throes of death. (Romans 1:16) C.H. Spurgeon stated, "It is well to preach as I do, with my lips; but you can all preach with your feet, and by your lives, and that is the most effective preaching. The preaching of holy lives is living preaching. The most effective ministry from a pulpit is that which is supported by godliness from the pew." (Spurgeon, "Kept Iniquity") R.A. Torrey declared, "I would rather win souls than be the greatest King or Emperor on earth; I would rather win souls than be the greatest general that ever commanded an army; I would rather win souls than be the greatest poet, or novelist, or literary man who ever walked this earth. My one ambition in life is to win as many as possible. Oh, it is the only thing worth doing, to save souls, and men and women – we can all do it!" (Martin 189)

A son fell out of a boat and cried to his father, "Throw me a rope." The dad threw the only rope he had to his son. The son cried, 'Dad, the rope is too short. Throw me a longer rope." There was no longer rope to be thrown. The boy's last words to his dad were, "Dad, the rope's too short; throw me a longer rope." God is saying to Christians "Throw out a longer rope to those perishing in the lake of sin." Let us resolve to throw out a longer rope, to increase our efforts, and to expend our energies in reaching the unsaved.

NEGLECT NOT STEWARDSHIP

"Now concerning the collection for the saints, as I have given order to the churches of Galatia, even so do ye. Upon the first *day* of the week let every one of you lay by him in store, as *God* hath prospered him, that there be no gatherings when I come." (1 Corinthians 16:1-2) "The liberal soul shall be made fat and he that watereth shall be watered also himself." (Proverbs 11:25) Water God's garden with monetary offerings and God will water your garden financially or otherwise. (2 Corinthians 9: 6-7) You say you cannot afford to give, but God says you cannot afford not to give. Don't neglect giving of your tithes and offerings to the Lord. (Malachi 3:10) There is a story of three quarters that teaches the lesson "little is much when God is in it." The story goes that three quarters were talking amongst themselves about how they were to be used. The first quarter said, "I'm going to be used to buy some candy for Jimmy to make him happy." The second quarter said, "I'm going to buy Timmy some marbles to make him happy." The third quarter said, "I'm going to be put into the offering plate by Tommy to help purchase a truck for a missionary." The other quarters laughed saying, "What can one little quarter do to buy a truck that costs $20,000?" In time enough money was raised to buy the truck. How does this story of the three quarters end? The candy purchased with the first quarter for Jimmy disappeared quickly. The marbles bought with the second quarter for Timmy were soon lost. However, the quarter given by Tommy to buy the truck was still at work years later delivering materials to missionary outposts. Where will you put your quarter? The writer of Hebrews exhorts, "Let us, then, always offer praise to God as our sacrifice through Jesus, which is the offering presented by lips that confess him as Lord. Do not forget to do good and to help one another, because these are the sacrifices that please God." (Hebrews 13: 15-16, GNT) Stewardship involves not only the proper use of the believer's treasure but his time and talent. (Romans 12: 1-2)

NEGLECT NOT SELF-EXAMINATION

With David, the Christian often should pray, "Search me, O God" (Psalm 139:23-24) regarding his heart and walk with Christ to detect sin, spiritual laxity or heresy. Spiritual physicals are imperative to assure spiritual health. Leonard Ravenhill wrote,

There is sin in the camp, there is treason today.
Is it in me? Is it in me, O Lord?
There's cause in our ranks for defeat and delay
Is it in me, is it in me O Lord?
Something of selfishness, garments or gold,
Something of hindrance in young and in old.
Something as to why God's blessing He doth withhold.
Is it in me, is it in me, is it in me, O Lord?
(Ravenhill 54)

The Christian should endeavor to live that he may declare with Charles A. Tindley,

Nothing between my soul and the Savior,
So that His blessed face may be seen;
Nothing preventing the least of His favor,
Keep the way clear! Let nothing between.

In the event of moral or spiritual failure God stands ready to graciously forgive, cleanse, and restore as with the prodigal son, David, and myriads of others. (I John 1: 7-9) Jeremy Camp is right in stating, "He'll take you back." Always!

NEGLECT NOT DAILY DYING TO SELF

The Apostle Paul said, "I die daily." (I Corinthians 15:31) If a giant such as Paul had to crawl upon the altar of death to self each day, how much more do you and I? The flesh will constantly seek to retake the throne in the believer's life, and thus every single day the first order of business is to crucify the flesh and its inordinate desires. (Romans 6: 6 – 13; John 12:24) There must be that daily presentation of the Christian's total self to the Lordship of Christ that he may be a Romans 12: 1-2 Christian. C.H. Spurgeon exhorts, "Walk worthy of your high calling and dignity. Remember, O Christian, that thou art a son of the King of kings. Therefore, keep thyself unspotted from the world. Soil not the fingers which are soon to sweep celestial strings; let not these eyes become the windows of lust which are soon to see the King in his beauty-let not those feet be defiled in miry places, which are soon to walk the golden streets-let not those hearts be filled with pride and bitterness which are ere long to be filled with heaven, and to overflow with ecstatic joy." (Spurgeon, Morning, September 11)

NEGLECT NOT SERVICE

Paul's council to young Timothy is to every believer, "Neglect not the gift that is in you" but stir it up to full flame.

(I Timothy 4:14) Believers have at least one gift to use in service to Christ. (Romans 12: 4-8; I Corinthians 12: 27-31; Ephesians 4:11-13) It may be (among others) the gift of exhortation (preaching), administration, hospitality, of helps, or of music and singing. Discover your gift(s) and operate within its realm in Christian service for greatest effectiveness. Fan, develop, and sharpen your gift(s) for its greatest usefulness. Never cease to improve the service you render unto Christ. "If I were fruitless," wrote John Bunyan, "it mattered not who commended me; if I were fruitful, I cared not who did condemn." (Bunyan 81) S.D. Gordon stated, "Long years ago, in the days before steam navigation, an ocean vessel came from a long voyage, up St. George's Channel, headed for Liverpool. When the pilot was taken on board, he cried abruptly to the captain, "What do you mean? You've let her drift off toward the Welsh coast, toward the shallows. Muster the crew." The crew was quickly mustered, and the pilot told of the danger in a few short words, and then said sharply, "Boys, it's death or deep water: hoist the mainsail." And only by dint of hardest work was the ship saved. If I could get the ear of the Church today I would, as a great kindness to it, cry out with all the earnestness of soul I could command, "*It's death or deep water*: deep water in the holy service of changing the world or death from foundering." (Gordon 155)

NEGLECT NOT THE SECOND COMING

Paul writes, "Looking for that blessed hope, and the glorious appearing of the great God and our Savior Jesus Christ, who gave Himself for us." (Titus 2:13). Have you been waiting, working, and watching with expectancy for Christ's coming? Prior to going to bed each night, the last action of Dr. Horatius Bonar, Scottish preacher and hymnwriter, was to draw back the drapes and look into the starry sky, asking, "Perhaps tonight, Lord?" Similarly Bonar's first action each morning was to lift the blind and look out on the morning dawn asking, "Perhaps today, Lord?' As Bonar, in an effort not to *neglect* the second coming of Christ I discipline myself each morning to spread my arms toward the heavens saying, "Lord today help me to look for your appearing and live accordingly." H. A. Ironside commented, "To profess to hold the doctrine of the premillennial coming of Christ is one thing. To be really held by it is quite another. He whose life is unrighteous, whose spirit is worldly, and whose outlook on life is carnal and selfish has never yet learned to love His appearing." (Great Preaching on Judgment 109) Early saints would keep this doctrine cognizant both in their minds and that of others by sharing the greeting, "Maranatha, Maranatha" ("The Lord comes. The Lord comes"). (Revelation 22:20) May Christians likewise do the same today.

A FINAL APPEAL

As you leave the pages of this study, embrace each of these *"Neglect Not's"* of spiritual growth that you may "Therefore, my beloved brethren, be ye steadfast, unmovable, always abounding in the work of the Lord, forasmuch as ye know that your labor is not in vain in the Lord." (I Corinthians 15:58) Growth is not optional to the believer. It is an imperative to maintain fellowship with Christ, focus upon Christ, freedom in Christ, and faithfulness to Christ. You will never outgrow the need to grow spiritually until gowned with His likeness in Heaven.

Digging Deeper

What are the ten *"Neglect Not's"* stated in this chapter? Why is their observance imperative to spiritual growth and effective ministry?

BIBLIOGRAPHY

Adler, Bill. Ask Billy Graham. Nashville: Thomas Nelson, 2007.

Augustine, St. Augustin on the Holy Trinity, Doctrinal Treatises and Moral Treatises: Nicene and Post-Nicene Fathers of the Christian Church Part 3. Whitefish, Montana: Kessinger Publishing, 2004.

Autrey, C.E. You Can Win Souls. Nashville: Broadman Press, 1961.

Baptist Faith and Message. 2000. <sbc.net/bfm/bfm2000. asp>.

Barber, Wayne. "Ephesians 4:11-13: Preserving the Unity of the Spirit, Part 3." <preceptaustin>.

Bisagno, John. The Power of Positive Praying (Preface). Grand Rapids: Zondervan Books, 1972.

Booth, William. "Duty." <jglm2atomicshops.com/dutywb. html>.

Bounds, E.M. Purpose in Prayer. LuLu.com, 2007.

Bounds, E.M. E.M. Bounds on Prayer. New Kensington, Pennsylvania: Whitaker House, 1997.

Bounds, Edward D. Power Through Prayer. Cosimo, Inc., 2007.

Bridges, Jerry. I Give You Glory, O God. Waterville, Maine: Thorndike Press, 2002.

Bright, Bill. "Your Personal Guide to Fasting and Prayer." <ccci.org/growth/growing-closer-to-god/how-to-fast/index.aspx – 15k>.

Brooks, Thomas and Alexander Balloch Grosart. The Complete Works of Thomas Brooks. Edinburgh: J. Nichol, 1866.

Bunyan, John. Grace Abounding to the Chief of Sinners. Whitefish, Montana: Kessinger Publishing, 2004.

Calvin, Jean, A. W. Morrison, David Wishart Torrance, Thomas Forsyth Torrance, Thomas Henry Louis Parker. A Harmony of the Gospels, Matthew, Mark and Luke. Grand Rapids: Wm. B. Eerdmans Publishing, 1995.

Carson, D.A. A Call to Spiritual Reformation. Grand Rapids: Baker Book House, 1992.

Chafer, Lewis S. Systematic Theology. Grand Rapids: Kregel Publications, 1993.

Chambers, Oswald. My Utmost for His Highest (May 10). Grand Rapids: Discovery House, 1992.

Chapman, J. Wilbur. "And Peter." Grand Rapids: Fleming H. Revell Company, 1896.

<thechurchonline.com/finance_business_tithing>. Crown Financial Ministries. C.H. Spurgeon. Business Tithing article.

Coleman, Robert E. The Master Plan of Evangelism. Old Tappan, New Jersey: Fleming H. Revell Company, 1988.

Coleridge, Samuel Taylor. The Complete Works of Samuel Taylor Coleridge. New York: Harper & Brothers, 1853.

Comfort, Philip and Walter Elwell. Tyndale Bible Dictionary. Carol Stream, Illinois: Tyndale House Publishers, 2001.

Comfort, Ray. Evidence Bible. Gainesville, Florida: Bridge-Logos Publishers, 2002.

Council on Foundations. "Quotations on Philanthropy & Giving." <cof.org/learn/content.cfm?ItemNumber=8 62&navItemNumber=2264>.

Courson, Jon. Courson's Application Commentary. Nashville: Nelson Publishing Company, 2004.

Cowman, L. B. Streams in the Desert. Grand Rapids: Zondervan, 1997.

Criswell, W.A. The Criswell Study Bible. Nashville: Nelson Publishing Company, 1979.

Criswell, W.A. "Satan" (Sermon February 26, 1956).

Criswell, W.A. "St. Patrick Was a Baptist Preacher" (March 16, 1958), The W.A. Criswell Sermon Library. <wacriswell.com>.

Criswell, W.A. Why I Preach that the Bible is Literally True. Nashville: Broadman Press, 1969.

Crown Financial Ministries. "Giving to Missions Work." <crown.org/LIBRARY/ViewArticle.aspx?ArticleId= 405>.

The Daily Study Bible Series. Philadelphia: Westminster Press, 2000.

D.L. Moody Year Book: A Living Daily Message from the Words of D.L. Moody. Kessinger Publishing, 1900.

De Gruchy, John W. The Cambridge Companion to Dietrich Bonhoeffer. New York: Cambridge University Press, 1999.

DeVoss, Rich. "Hope for My Heart: Ten Lessons for Life," The Evidence Bible, Ron Comfort, Ed., Gainesville, Florida: Bridge-Logos Publishers, 2002.

Dixon, Francis W. What Every Christian Should Know. Landsdowne Bible School and Postal Fellowship: England: Bournemouth, June 9, 1964.

Douglas, J.D., Ed. The Work of the Evangelist. Minneapolis: World Wide Publishers, 1984.

Drummond, Lewis A. The Evangelist. Lubbock, Texas: Word Publishing, 2001.

Edwards, Jonathan. The Experience that Counts! N.R. Needham, Ed., London: Grace Publications Trust, 1991.

Elwell, Walter A., Ed. Evangelical Dictionary of the Bible. Grand Rapids: Baker Book House, 2001.

Encarta Book of Quotations. New York: Macmillian, 2000.

Enns. The Moody Handbook of the Bible. Chicago: Moody Press, 1997.

Evangelical Dictionary of the Bible. Walter A. Elwell, Ed. Grand Rapids: Baker Book House, 2001.

Expository Dictionary of Bible Words. Grand Rapids: Zondervan, 1985.

Fordham, Keith. Personal Correspondence, 20 December, 2008.

Fordham, Keith. Evangelism Born in the Heart of God. Fayeteville, Georgia: KFEA, 2002.

Geisler, Norman. Systematic Theology, Vol. 2. Minneapolis: Bethany House, 2003.

Geisler, Norman. Systematic Theology, Vol. 3. Minneapolis: Bethany House, 2004.

George, Andrew Jackson. The Complete Poetical Works of William Wordsworth. Boston & New York: Houghton, Mifflin & Co., 1904.

Goldsworthy, Graeme. According to Plan. Nottingham, England: Intervarsity Press, 1991.

Gordon, S. D. What It will Take to Change the World. Grand Rapids: Baker, 1979.

Graham, Billy. Life Wisdom from Billy Graham. Kansas: Hallmark Books, 2006

Graham, Billy. Rules for Christian Living. Charlotte, North Carolina: Billy Graham Evangelistic Association, 1953.

Great Preaching on Christ, Vol. 19. Murfreesboro, Tennessee: Sword of the Lord Publishers, 2002.

Great Preaching on Judgment. Vol. 15. Murfreesboro, Tennessee: Sword of the Lord Publishers, Vol. 15, 1990.

Havner, Vance. Messages on Revival. Grand Rapids: Baker Book House, 1958.

<helives.com/blog/2007/09/17/convicting-spurgeon-quote>.

Henry, Matthew. Matthew Henry Commentary Vol. 3. New Tappan, New Jersey: Fleming H. Revell Company, undated, ca. 1970.

Henry, Matthew. Matthew Henry Commentary on the Whole Bible. Peabody, Massachusetts: Hendrickson Publishers, 1991.

Henry, Matthew, and Philip Henry. The Miscellaneous Works of the Rev. Matthew Henry. Robinson, 1833.

Hughes, Kent. "Grace of Giving" (Sermon). <PreachingTodaySermons.com>.

Johnson, Marshall D. The Evolution of Christianity: Twelve Crises that Shaped the Church. Continuum International Publishing Group, 2005.

Johnston, Thomas P. The Gift of the Evangelist and Revival. (unpublished notes).

a' Kempis, Thomas. Imitation of Christ. Peabody, Massachusetts: Hendrickson Publishers, July 30, 2004.

Lawrence, Robert R. The Evidence Bible, Ron Comfort, Ed. Gainesville, Florida: Bidge-Logos Publishers, 2002.

Lee, R.G. "Christ Above All," Great Preaching on Christ, Vol. 19. Murfreesboro, Tennessee: Sword of the Lord Publishers, 2002.

Lewis, C.S. The Complete C.S. Lewis Signature Classics. New York: HarperCollins Publishers, 2002.

Lewis, C.S. Sermon-Central.Com

Little, Paul. Know What You Believe. Wheaton, Illinois: Victor Books, 1979.

Lloyd-Jones, Martyn. The Christian Soldier. Grand Rapids: Baker, 1977.

Lorentzen, Melvin E., Ed. Evangelistic Preaching. Minneapolis: World Wide Publications, 1990.

Lucado, Max. Life Lessons-Book of Psalms (Preface). Lubbock, Texas: Word Publishing, 1997.

Lucado, Max. For These Tough Times. Nashville: Thomas Nelson, 2006.

Lucado, Max. And the Angels were Silent. Sisters, Oregon: Multnomah Books, 2003.

Luther, Martin. <thinkexist.com/quotation/I_often_laugh_ at_satan-and_there_is_nothing_that/166764.html>.

MacArthur, John. "Beware of the Pretenders: The Eternal Security of the Christian" (Sermon). <biblebb. com>.

MacArthur, John. A Faith To Grow On. Nashville: Thomas Nelson, 2000.

MacArthur, John. How to Meet the Enemy. Wheaton, Illinois: Victory Books, 1992.

MacArthur, John. The MacArthur Study Bible. Nashville: Nelson Publishers, 1997.

MacArthur, John. Truth Matters. Nashville: Nelson Publishers, 2004.

MacDonald, Gordon. <generousgiving.org>.

MacDonald and Farstad. Believer's Bible Commentary: Old and New Testaments. Nashville: Thomas Nelson, 1995.

Mahaney, C.J. Humility: True Greatness. New York: Multnomah Publishing, 2005.

Martin, Roger. R.A. Torrey: Apostle of Certainty. Murfreesboro, Tennessee: Sword of the Lord Publishers, 2000.

Matthews, C.E. The Southern Baptist Program of Evangelism. Nashville: Convention Press, 1956.

Moody, D.L. The D.L. Moody Book: A Living Daily Message from the Words of D.L. Moody. New York: Fleming H. Revell, 1900.

Moody, D.L. Great Preaching on the Second Coming, Vol. 11. Murfreesboro, Tennessee: Sword of the Lord Publishers, 1989.

Moody, D.L. Great Preaching on Soul Winning, Vol. 13. Murfreesboro, Tennessee: Sword of the Lord Publishers, 1989.

Moody, D.L. Prevailing Prayer: what Hinders It?: What Hinders It?, Chicago: Fleming H. Revell, 1884.

Moody, D.L. Pleasures and Profit in Bible Study. Grand Rapids: Fleming Revell Publishers, 1895.

Moody, D.L. <quotationsbook.com/quote/6710/ - 18k>.

Moody, D.L. <thinkexist.com/quotes/dwight_l_moody/2. html – 31k>.

Moody, D.L. <vsb.gospelcom.net/rom12.html – 19k>.

Moody, D.L. "The Way to God and How to Find It." <whatsaiththescripture.com/Voice/Moody>.

Murray, Andrew. Waiting on God. New Kensington, Pennsylvania: Whitaker House, 1983.

Murray, Andrew. With Christ in the School of Prayer. New Kensington, Pennsylvania: Whitaker House, 1981.

Newell, William R. Romans: Verse-By-Verse: Verse-by-Verse. Grand Rapids: Kregel Publications, 2004.

Myra, Harold Lawrence and Marshall Shelley. The Leadership Secrets of Billy Graham. Grand Rapids: Zondervan, 2005.

Our Daily Bread. June 27, 2004. Grand Rapids: Radio Bible Class.

Packer, J.I. Concise Theology: A Guide to Historic Christian Beliefs. Wheaton, Illinois: Tyndale House, 1993.

Packer, J.I. Growing in Christ. Wheaton, Illinois: Crossway Books, 1994.

Pierson, A.T. George Mueller of Bristol. Grand Rapids: Fleming Revell Company, 1899.

Pink, A.W. The Attributes of God. Grand Rapids: Baker Books, 1991.

Pink, A.W. Profiting from the Word. Edinburgh, Scotland: Banner of Truth Trust, 1970.

Piper, John. "The Agonizing Problem of the Assurance of Salvation." <new-testament-christian.com/eternal-security>.

Prayer and Intercession Quotes. <tentmaker.org>.

Rainer, Thom. The Baptist Courier. May 1, 2008.

Ravenhill, Leonard. Why Revival Tarries. Grand Rapids: Bethany House Publishers, 2004.

<realmoffaith.org/lifeoffaith.htm>.

Rice, John R. Rice Reference Bible. Nashville: Nelson Publishing, 1981.

Ryle, J.C. "Holiness" Sermon. <iclnet.org/pub/resources/text/history/spurgeon/web/ryle.holiness.html – 49k>.

Ryrie Study Bible. Chicago: Moody Press, 1994.

<servantsheartfelllowship.blogspot.com/ - 75k>.

<sermoncentral.com/print_friend.asp?ContributorID=&SermonID=125271>.

Simmonds, James D. Milton Studies 18. Pittsburgh, Pennsylvania: University of Pittsburgh Press, 1990.

Smith, Bailey. Real Evangelism. Nashville: Broadman Press, 1978.

Smith, Harold J. Fast Your Way to Health. Nashville: Nelson Publishers, 1979.

Smith, William. Smith's Bible Dictionary. Peabody, Massachusetts: Hendrickson, 1990.

Spurgeon, C. H. The Treasury of David Vol 1 . Byron Center, Michigan: Associated Publishers and Authors, Inc., 1970.

Spurgeon, C. H. "The Ascension of Christ" (Sermon 0982, March 26, 1871). Metropolitan Tabernacle Pulpit. Pasadena, Texas: Pilgrim Publications, 1976.

Spurgeon, C. H., Susannah Spurgeon, and Joseph Harrald. The Autobiography of Charles H. Spurgeon. Revell Publishers, 1898.

Spurgeon, C. H. Sermons of Rev. C.H. Spurgeon of London. New York: R.Carter & Brothers, 1885.

Spurgeon, C. H. An All-Round Ministry: Addresses to Ministers and Students. BiblioBazaar, LLC, 2008.

Spurgeon, C. H. "The Comer's Conflict with Satan," Spurgeon's Sermons Vol 2. Grand Rapids: Baker Books, 1999.

Spurgeon, C.H. "A Cheerful Giver Is Beloved of God" (Sermon 835, August 27, 1868). Metropolitan Tabernacle Pulpit. Pasadena, Texas: Pilgrim Publications, 1976.

Spurgeon, C. H. "A Best Donation" (Sermon 2234, April 5, 1891). Metropolitan Tabernacle Pulpit. Pasadena, Texas: Pilgrim Publications, 1976.

Spurgeon, C.H. "The Dying Thief in a New Light" (Sermon 1881, August 23, 1885). Metropolitan Tabernacle Pulpit. Pasadena, Texas: Pilgrim Publications, 1976.

Spurgeon, C.H. The Early Years: C.H. Spurgeons' Autobiography. London: Banner of Truth, 1962.

Spurgeon, C.H. "Heirs of God" (Sermon 2961, July 22, 1875). Metropolitan Tabernacle Pulpit. Pasadena, Texas: Pilgrim Publications, 1976.

Spurgeon, C.H. "The Holy Ghost – The Great Teacher" (Sermon 50, November 18, 1855). Metropolitan Tabernacle Pulpit. Pasadena, Texas: Pilgrim Publications, 1976.

Spurgeon, C.H. "How to Read the Bible" (Sermon 1503, 1879). Metropolitan Tabernacle Pulpit. Pasadena, Texas: Pilgrim Publications, 1976.

Spurgeon, C.H. "Joining the Church" (Sermon 3411). Metropolitan Tabernacle Pulpit. Pasadena, Texas: Pilgrim Publications, 1976.

Spurgeon, C.H. "Kept From Iniquity" (Sermon 2432, September 29, 1895). Metropolitan Tabernacle Pulpit. Pasadena, Texas: Pilgrim Publications, 1976.

Spurgeon, C.H. Morning and Evening. Great Britain: Christian Focus Publications, 1994.

Spurgeon, C.H. "Particular Redemption" (Sermon 0181, February 28, 1858). Metropolitan Tabernacle Pulpit. Pasadena, Texas: Pilgrim Publications, 1976.

Spurgeon, C.H. A Puritan Catechism. What is Sanctification?. <grace.org.uk/faith/spurgeon>.

Spurgeon, C.H., W.R. Nicoll, and Godfrey Holden Pike. Sermons of Rev. C.H. Spurgeon, Second Series. Sheldon, 1869.

Spurgeon, C.H. "Sin: Its Spring-Head, Stream, and Sea" (Sermon 2204, May 10, 1891). Metropolitan Tabernacle Pulpit. Pasadena, Texas: Pilgrim Publications, 1976.

Spurgeon, C.H. "Solitude, Silence and Submission" (Sermon 2468, June 13, 1886). Metropolitan Tabernacle Pulpit. Pasadena, Texas: Pilgrim Publications, 1976.

Spurgeon, C.H. The Soulwinner. New Kensington, Pennsylvania: Whitaker House, 1995.

Spurgeon, C.H. Spurgeon's Gems. New York: Sheldon, Blakeman & Co., 1959.

Steadman, Ray C. "The Church's Building and Maintenance Service" (Sermon). Palo Alto, California: Discovery Publishing, 1976.

Steadman, Ray C. "If God Be For Us" (Sermon). Palo Alto, California: Discovery Publishing, 1976.

Stevenson, H.F., Ed. "God's Man: Studies in 2 Timothy." The Keswick Week 1969. London: Marshall, Morgan, and Scott, 1969.

Stott, John. The Bible and the Crisis of Authority. London: Falcon, 1972.

Stott, John. Culture and the Bible. Downers Grove: IVP, 1981.

Stott, John. "InterVarsity's Student Leadership," Maintaining Spiritual Freshness. Winter 1992.

Stott, John. The Letters of John: Tyndale New Testament Commentaries. Revised Edition. Grand Rapids: Eerdmans, 1988.

Stott, John. The Message of Galatians. London and Downers Grove: IVP, 1968.

Stott, John. The Message of 2 Timothy. London and Downers Grove: IVP, 1973.

Stott, John. The Preacher's Portrait. London: Tyndale Press, 1961.

Stott, John. You Can Trust the Bible. Grand Rapids: Discovery House, 1991.

Stott, John. The Contemporary Christian. Downers Grove, Illinois: Intervarsity Press, 1995.

Taylor, Hudson. <puritanfellowshipo.com/2008/07james-hudson-taylor-powerful-quotes-on>.

Taylor, Jack. Victory Over the Devil (Foreword by Stephen Olford). Nashville: Broadman Press, 1973.

The South in the Building of the Nation. Southern Historical Publication Society, 1909.

Trent, John Scott. Evangelists in Action. Orlando, Florida: Daniels Publishers, 1971.

Tomkins, Stephen. John Wesley: A Biography. Grand Rapids: Eerdmans Publishing, 2003.

Today in the Word. July 2000. Moody Bible Institute. <today-intheword.com>.

Tozer, A.W. The Pursuit of Man. <unbreakablejoy.blogspot. com/2008/03/Nicole-mullen-my-redeemer-lives>.

<uncleernest.com/evangelize.htm>.

Warden, Michael D. "The Discipline of Solitude." <lifeway. com/lwc/article>.

Warfield, B.B. The Formation of the Canon of the New Testament. Philadelphia: American Sunday School Union, 1982.

Whitney, Donald S. Spiritual Disciplines of the Christian Life. Colorado Springs: NavPress, 2002.

Whitsell, Faris. Basic Evangelism. Grand Rapids: Zondervan, 1949.

Wiersbe, Warren. The Best of A.W. Tozer. Grand Rapids: Baker Book House, 1978.

Wiersbe, Warren. Wiersbe's Expository Commentary on the New Testament. Wheaton, Illinois: SP Publications, 1992.

Wiersbe, Warren. The Stragety of Satan. Wheaton, Illinois: Tyndale House, 1979.

WordAlive. Wycliffe Bible Translators of Canada. Fall 2007, Vol. 25 Number 3.

Zuck, Roy B. The Speaker's Quote Book. Grand Rapids: Kregel Publications, 1997.

CPSIA information can be obtained
at www.ICGtesting.com
Printed in the USA
BVHW031959100419
545205BV00001B/4/P

9 781607 912965